Tax Tips for Property Developers and Renovators

By

Lee Sharpe

Publisher Details
This guide is published by Tax Portal Ltd. 3 Sanderson Close, Great Sankey, Warrington, Cheshire, WA5 3LN.

'Tax Tips for Property Developers and Renovators' – First published **'Tax Secrets For Property Developers and Renovators'** in July 2006. Second edition April 2007.Third edition May 2008. Fourth edition May 2009. Fifth edition August 2010. Sixth edition May 2011. Seventh edition April 2012. Eighth edition May 2013. Ninth edition April 2014. Tenth edition April 2015. Eleventh edition April 2016.Twelfth edition April 2017. Thirteenth edition April 2018.Fourteenth edition March 2019. Fifteenth Edition May 2020. Sixteenth edition April 2021. Seventeenth edition April 2022. Eighteenth edition April 2023.

A CIP Copy of this guide is available from the British Library.

978-1-7394153-3-4

Disclaimer

1. This guide is produced for General guidance only, and professional advice should be sought before any decision is made. Individual circumstances can vary and therefore no responsibility can be accepted by the author, Lee Sharpe, or the publisher Tax Portal Ltd, for any action taken, or any decision made to refrain from action, by any readers of this guide.

2. Tax rules and legislation are constantly changing and therefore the information printed in this guide is correct at the time of printing – April 2023.

3. Neither the author nor Tax Portal Ltd offer financial, legal or investment advice. If you require such advice, then we urge you to seek the opinion of an appropriate professional in the relevant field. We care about your success and therefore encourage you to take appropriate advice before you put any of your financial or other resources at risk. Don't forget, investment values can decrease as well as increase.

4. To the fullest extent permitted by law, Lee Sharpe and Tax Portal Ltd do not accept liability for any direct, indirect, special, consequential or other losses or damages of whatsoever kind arising from using this guide.

   The guide itself is provided 'as is' without express or implied warranty.

5. Lee Sharpe and Tax Portal Ltd reserve the right to alter any part of this guide at any time without notice.

Contents

About Lee Sharpe

Lee is a Chartered Tax Adviser and tax consultant with over twenty years' experience in helping individuals, families, businesses and advisers with their tax affairs.

Lee writes extensively on tax matters for taxpayers and their advisers, including through the Tax Insider publications, Bloomsbury Professional and the TaxationWeb website. He also lectures taxpayers, accountants and other financial advisers on tax issues.

While he has appeared on TV to comment on tax matters, it was only long enough to establish that he really has a face for radio, and to give fellow members of his local CIOT branch sufficient ammunition with which to embarrass him at committee meetings.

When he is not giving tax advice or writing about tax matters, he is busy looking after his two children – not because he likes them, but because he wants to make sure that his office is not used exclusively for business purposes…

1 About This Guide

In recent years, there has been a great increase in interest in the property market, and this guide offers advice on the tax pitfalls and opportunities for those who are involved in this dynamic sector.

In particular, it is aimed at the following three categories:

1.1 Homeowners

All of us who own our own homes hope we are sitting on a goldmine! For many people, their home is their most valuable asset – for some, it is their pension fund.

This section of the guide looks at the tax breaks available to homeowners, and how to get the maximum benefit from them. It also warns of traps for the unwary!

It is not unusual for a homeowner to find themselves becoming a property developer, perhaps by building another property on their land, or by receiving an offer from a developer to buy their home. We will look at the (sometimes unexpected) ways that such projects are taxed by HM Revenue and Customs (referred to in this guide from now on as HMRC).

1.2 Buy to Let

It might seem that these days, almost everyone is a landlord. In truth it's not *quite* almost everyone, but they do make up a very significant minority, at least: HMRC reported that just under **3million** 2019/20 tax returns included property income – and this figure excludes those landlords who dealt with modest rental incomes through the PAYE system for salary or wages, and those who otherwise do not need to complete a tax return. In this section, we shall look at the tax treatment of buy to let investors, both on the income from their properties, and on the sale of those properties. We shall cover the letting (and selling) of residential and commercial properties, and that interesting hybrid, furnished holiday accommodation.

1.3 Buy to Sell

Not everyone buys property in order to enjoy the rental income – many intend to turn the properties over quickly, by selling them again at a profit.

This sector can be further divided into three basic sub-categories, all of which we shall look at:

- "**Turnarounds"** These work on the basic commercial principle of "buy cheap and sell dear". A property is bought for a bargain price, perhaps at auction, and sold on almost immediately, with little or no work done on it to increase its value.
- **"Refurbs"** As the name implies, in a "Refurb", a run-down property is bought, then refurbished, and sold – or a large property is bought, converted into smaller units such as flats, and sold. Refurbs may be distinguished from Turnarounds by reason of the more substantive investment of time and money put into improving the property for onward sale.

- **"Property Development"** This can be more or less the same as a refurb, or it may involve buying a vacant plot of land and constructing a new building on it for sale.

1.4 Tax Rates and Devolved Taxes

Unless otherwise indicated, we shall be using 2023/24 rates and allowances. 2018/19 saw a significant divergence when comparing Scotland with the rest of the UK, as the Scottish government moved not just thresholds but introduced entirely new bands, and rates. Welsh Income Tax has also basically 'devolved' from the rest of the UK since April 2019. However, Wales' National Assembly has so far decided **not** to move away from standard "rest-of-UK" rates and bands.

Interestingly for tax geeks, the Scottish and Welsh devolved taxing powers basically cannot affect savings income (including dividends) so that the Scottish (and Welsh) Higher Rate thresholds for bank interest, dividends and the like will be £50,270 in 2023/24, just like the rest of the UK – which potentially makes for some quirky calculations around the c£40,000 - c£50,000 income band for Scottish taxpayers, depending on the mix of incomes at that level.

There are also potential knock-on implications, such as eligibility for the 'new' Marriage Allowance. However, it should be emphasised that in very many cases, 'devolved' taxpayers (including Welsh taxpayers, as and when thresholds, etc., diverge), will end up with similar results to rest-of-UK taxpayers and, even where they do not, the differences are likely to be relatively modest. **This book will apply the 'standard' UK rates and thresholds throughout.**

1.5 Stamp Taxes

The Scottish tax regime also includes "Land and Buildings Transaction Tax" (LBTT) instead of the Stamp Duty Land Tax (SDLT) with which most readers will be familiar. Since 1 April 2018, "Land Transaction Tax" has been payable in Wales, instead of SDLT. While very similar, there are differences between the three regimes, and **readers operating in Scotland or Wales should get specific advice on LBTT and LTT respectively**; this guide follows the SDLT regime such as it applies in the rest of the UK (i.e., England and Northern Ireland).

2 A Word About Limited Companies

This guide predominantly focuses on the taxation of individuals who own property, or trade in property, as sole traders, co-owners/joint investors, or as members of a partnership.

In some cases, it can be advantageous to use a limited company as the vehicle for investing or trading in property – the commonest examples being:

- If you are hoping to avoid the new Draconian rules that restrict tax relief on mortgage interest for residential lettings undertaken by individuals (and other persons subject to Income Tax)

- If you don't "need" the extra income, so intend to plough the profits from the rental business back into buying more rental properties, rather than to draw them out for personal expenditure

- If you are looking to facilitate the transfer of wealth to younger generations, such as to children and grandchildren

- If you are a property developer, looking to limit your potential exposure to claims against the rest of your assets

The decision whether to use a company or not can become quite involved, and it is beyond the scope of this guide. However, we do occasionally consider how things work differently in a company, to try to give you a better overall appreciation of the *pros* and *cons* of working for yourself, or through your own company.

If you would like detailed information and advice about whether a limited company would be the best way forward for your business, our guide "**How to Use Companies to Reduce Property Taxes**" is available from www.property-tax-portal.co.uk. Between the two publications, they offer a comprehensive guide to tax for the property investor or the property trader.

3 What This Guide is Not About

All of the tax strategies in this guide are legitimate ways of planning to minimise your tax liabilities.

In some cases, tax planning can involve "grey areas" of the tax legislation, where there is more than one way to interpret the law, and should this be the case in this publication, it will be clearly indicated in the text.

This guide is not about complicated tax avoidance schemes, many of which do not work, or are vulnerable to retrospective (or retroactive) legislation.

It is most emphatically **not** about ways to evade tax – that is, to reduce your tax bill dishonestly by telling the taxman less than the whole truth.

The above may seem obvious, but we mention it because we have sometimes been quite surprised by the advice taxpayers tell us they have received from other sources – in some cases, if they had followed that advice, they would have been straying over the line that separates (legal) tax avoidance from (criminal) tax evasion – a line that was famously described by Dennis Healey, the former Chancellor of the Exchequer, as having "the thickness of a prison wall".

This distinction is so important that we will begin by looking at what separates tax planning, tax avoidance, and tax evasion.

4 Staying on the Right Side of the Prison Wall ("Tax Compliance")

"The thickness of a prison wall" – the difference between tax planning, tax avoidance, and tax evasion, and why it matters!

Taxation has rather murky origins – arguably, it began when a party of Norman soldiers rode into an English village, and stole all the chickens.

Perhaps one of the earliest examples of tax planning (or maybe tax avoidance, depending on your point of view) would have been hiding some of your chickens when you heard the approaching hoof beats.

As things got more sophisticated, both the way taxes were charged and the ways they were avoided became more complicated.

You can still see the bricked-up windows on old houses (done to avoid the 18th century Window Tax). It has been suggested that the first Lurchers (a delightful breed of dog: a cross between a greyhound and a pastoral breed such as a Border Collie) were bred to avoid the luxury tax on Greyhounds – in 1823, for example, the annual tax on a Greyhound was £1, whereas for any other breed of dog, it was only 8 shillings (40p).

If we fast forward to the present, the way the law now stands on trying to reduce your tax bill works broadly like this:

4.1 Tax Planning and the Duke's Gardener

In 1935, the House of Lords gave their judgement in the case of the Duke of Westminster, who had set up a tax planning scheme involving his gardener (and other employees) and a Deed of Covenant – the details do not matter, as sadly that particular scheme no longer works.

Their lordships said the Duke's scheme successfully reduced his tax bill, and added that:

"Every man is entitled if he can to order his affairs so that the tax attaching under the appropriate Acts is less than it otherwise would be".

This remains true today, though there have been developments since that have set some limits to this principle.

4.2 Targeted Anti-Avoidance Legislation

One of the reasons that the specific scheme used by the Duke of Westminster no longer works is that legislation was passed to prevent it from doing so in future.

For many years, this was the only way that the Government could counter tax avoidance schemes – by identifying how a specific scheme worked, and then passing legislation to ensure it was no longer effective.

One of the problems with this approach (from HMRC's point of view) is that it is always a couple of years or so behind the times, and by the time the law is on the statute book, a way round may already have been devised.

The other problem (from the taxpayer's point of view, this time) is that supposedly targeted anti-avoidance legislation can catch quite innocent transactions, or can apply in circumstances where the average taxpayer is simply unaware that the law exists, much less that it applies to him or to her!

There are several cases of this type of legislation in this guide – for example:

4.2.1 Construction Industry Scheme (CIS)

The "Construction Industry Scheme" as a whole, which broadly targets the entire construction industry in the UK, and basically requires property developers and contractors generally to deduct tax from certain payments to tradesmen, and keep records of payments to others (see 7.7).

4.2.2 Security Deposit Scheme(s)

The government has widened the scope of existing powers, to allow it to require businesses to deposit sums in advance of anticipated Construction Industry Scheme (CIS) liabilities and Corporation Tax liabilities (this is in addition to pre-existing powers to demand security deposits for VAT, and for PAYE/NIC payroll taxes). The extension of the security deposit regime to cover CIS deductions will be of particular relevance to property developers who fall within the scope of CIS (see 7.7 again).

The additional scope applies from April 2019, and will be triggered where HMRC perceives there to be a high risk that the taxpayer business will default on such payments. Typically, security deposits are requested where the director(s) of a company has also run a company that has previously become insolvent, owing significant sums to the Crown. Widening the scope will increase the fixed cost of entering the market, for those businesses that are caught. Failing to provide a security deposit can amount to a **criminal** offence. If HMRC tells you that you need to provide a security deposit, then take professional advice. For example, it may be possible to get the amount(s) reduced.

4.2.3 VAT Reverse Charge on Construction Services

In a further crackdown on those involved in the Construction Industry Scheme, (see 7.7), from 1 March 2021, some contractors are required to account for the VAT *they are charged* by sub-contractors within CIS. This effectively makes the payer responsible to HMRC for the VAT that would otherwise be accounted for by the billing business that is providing the service.

<u>Example</u>

> Lucinda has a small VAT-registered roofing business. She spends a month on a roofing job for a project management contractor company, and raises an invoice for £8,000. She is caught by the VAT Reverse Charge on Construction Services, so:
>
> She **cannot** charge output VAT on her invoice for £8,000, that would otherwise be
>
> £8,000 x 20% = £1,600
>
> She **does not** receive the VAT of £1,600 that would ordinarily be due
>
> But she still has to fund all of her own business' input VAT costs for materials, etc.

Lucinda will now likely end up with HMRC owing VAT to her every month on a rolling basis – which is the whole point of the new regime

Meanwhile, the larger project management company will "charge itself" for the VAT Lucinda would traditionally have charged, reducing its own VAT bill without any money having changed hands, and accounting to HMRC for the net amount as normal in its own VAT return (this assumes the project management company is at the top of the reverse charge chain)

Thankfully, this new Reverse Charge will **not** normally apply to most small and medium-sized property developers, because:

- It basically applies only to paying businesses that are themselves VAT-registered, and most property developers are not VAT-registered (unless they are large, build brand-new homes, or make VAT-taxable supplies for some other reason – see 7.7), and
- It does not apply in relation to zero-rated construction supplies (such as when building brand new homes), and
- It targets supplies from one building contractor to another, rather than to the end client, (usually the developer reading this book)

Even so, where a property developer thinks that the scope of their construction activity is so wide that their business may be caught, then they should seek advice, because the regime is complex and may require a serious overhaul of their accounting systems and, (and it is likely also to put a serious dent in their cashflow).

4.2.4 Transactions in Land Rules

The "Transactions in Land" rules, which can turn what you thought was going to be a small Capital Gains Tax bill into a large Income Tax bill. (Previously at Section 752 ITA 2007 but now spread across various parts of various tax acts after being 'souped up' by the 2016 Finance Act – see Chapter 6 for a whole chapter devoted to this legislative nut-cracking sledgehammer, and its limitations).

4.2.5 Making Directors/Shareholders Personally Liable for a Company's Debts

Finance Act 2020 introduced legislation to allow HMRC to make directors, other officers and shareholders "jointly and severally liable" for their company's tax debts to HMRC. This will allow HMRC to collect the company's entire tax debt from one or more individuals 'behind' the company – commonly referred to as "piercing the corporate veil".

HMRC already had some powers in this regard but historically, they could be applied only relatively narrowly, and the new proposals represent a significant enhancement of those powers – such as allowing HMRC to make individuals personally liable for tax debts that arose in companies that were insolvent up to 5 years ago.

Very simply, HMRC is able to apply the Liability Notice where:

(1) The company is insolvent, (or at risk of becoming so), and the company has engaged in tax avoidance or evasion activity, **or**

(2) The individual director or shareholder has been involved with 2 or more previous companies in broadly the same line of business, that have been

subject to insolvency procedures in the preceding 5 years, with aggregate tax debts to HMRC (in the 'old' companies) being more than £10,000, **or**

(3) The regime was extended to cover companies that received coronavirus support payments (e.g., under the Coronavirus Job Retention Scheme) *to which they were **not** entitled*, but HMRC expects to be unable to recover any excessive payment from the company

It follows that (1) is broadly meant to discourage companies from adopting tax-abusive behaviours while leaving insufficient funds in the company to make good any tax liabilities subsequently found to be due, while (2) is meant to prevent the repeated "phoenixing" of companies at the expense of the public purse; (3) has elements of both.

HMRC promises that, pandemic payments aside, the enhanced powers will be used only where there is tax avoidance, evasion or repeated non-payment of tax, and will not stifle enterprise in genuine commercial businesses. Just as with the enhanced security deposit legislation, (4.2.2 above), directors and shareholders who have been involved with companies that have previously become insolvent owing significant tax debts to the Crown may find that HMRC adopts a more aggressive attitude in relation to debt collection, leaving them more exposed, personally.

4.3 The "Ramsay" Doctrine

Since the early 1980s, the Courts have developed a new way of interpreting tax legislation (the name comes from one of the earliest cases on the subject, and has nothing to do with bad-tempered TV chefs). The Ramsay doctrine says that:

If a tax planning scheme involves a series of preordained steps, and one or more of those steps has no commercial purpose except to avoid tax, then that step can be ignored, and you look at the commercial reality of the transaction rather than the form it has been given by the scheme.

This way of looking at the law came about as a result of a number of highly artificial and complex schemes to avoid tax that were being marketed at the time.

The Ramsay doctrine is still evolving, and it is something that cannot be ignored when considering tax planning ideas. As a recent example, in **Khan v HMRC [2021] EWCA Civ 624**, it was actually the *taxpayer* who wanted the Ramsay principle to be applied to an unhelpfully strict interpretation of the transactions involved in that case – unsuccessfully, alas. The moral of the story is that you should always check your tax planning with a suitably qualified professional, to gauge whether or not it is likely to work as intended.

4.4 The DOTAS Disclosure Rules

In the last few years, legislation has been passed that requires those who market certain types of complex tax avoidance schemes to disclose the details to HMRC.

Anyone who then uses one of these schemes has to disclose the fact in their tax return. There are severe penalties for failure to comply with these rules.

This requirement to disclose such schemes has two consequences for those who decide to use them:

- They can be sure that HMRC will look very closely at the scheme to see if it is technically effective, and if it is not, they will have the names of everyone who is using the scheme

- Even if the scheme works, it is likely that legislation (sometimes retrospective) will be introduced to block the scheme.

None of the tax planning strategies described in this guide falls into this dangerous category of tax planning scheme, and none of them requires to be disclosed to HMRC in this way.

4.5 General Anti-Abuse Rule (GAAR)

Since the 2013 Finance Act we have also had a "General Anti-Abuse Rule" or "GAAR".

Essentially, this enables HMRC to take action against artificial tax-planning schemes that seek to achieve results not intended by the tax legislation. It is most **unlikely** to have any effect on the sort of tax planning described in this book, if HMRC are to be believed, because they offer the reassurance that the GAAR is aimed exclusively at the sort of highly artificial "contrived" tax schemes that would typically fall under the DOTAS "Disclosure Rules" described in 4.4 above.

4.6 Accelerated Payments and Follower Notices

The 2014 Finance Act contained two other measures that took effect from Royal Assent to the Act in the summer of 2014:

- "Accelerated payments" allow HMRC to serve notice on a taxpayer using a scheme disclosable under DOTAS (see above) or being countered by the GAAR, requiring them to pay the tax in dispute immediately, rather than waiting for the result of the dispute with HMRC

- "Follower notices" can be issued by HMRC to those using avoidance schemes "similar" to any scheme HMRC win their case against in court. A "follower notice" requires the taxpayer using the "similar" scheme to amend their tax return to give up the tax saving from the avoidance scheme, or face a penalty.

These measures are again aimed at what HMRC might term "artificial" or "contrived" arrangements, such as might be found in "disclosable" schemes as above. We do not expect anything that we recommend in this book to fall foul of these measures, either.

4.7 Special Penalties for Serial Tax Avoiders

Finance Act 2016 saw the introduction of a new regime designed to discourage taxpayers from repeatedly using tax avoidance schemes. Once a taxpayer has participated in a scheme that has been 'defeated' by HMRC, HMRC will issue a 'warning notice' to the taxpayer that lasts for 5 years. During that period, the taxpayer is obliged to provide detailed information about any other tax avoidance schemes that he or she has entered into. If a new tax avoidance scheme is then defeated, the taxpayer will have to pay additional penalties, which escalate up to 60% by the third such defeat. The taxpayer's details may also be published as a "Serial Tax Avoider", and access to ordinary direct tax reliefs may be restricted.

4.8 Tax Evasion – The Other Side of the Prison Wall!

Tax planning and tax avoidance are both entirely legal. Tax evasion is a criminal offence. Tax evasion pretty much always involves dishonesty in some form or other.

For example:

- In the days of the window tax, some houses were built with "dummy" windows made of bricks, or the windows in existing houses were removed and bricked up – the tax only applied to glass windows. That was tax planning.

- In other cases, houses were designed with one very large window where previously there might have been two or more small ones.

  We have heard of a case where an entire course of bricks made of glass linked all the windows on one wall of a house, and it was claimed they were all one window for the purposes of the tax.

  The tax commissioners refused to accept this argument and the tax had to be paid. That was tax avoidance, though unsuccessful.

- Some people bricked up their windows only when the "Surveyor" from the Inland Revenue was due to inspect the property.

  There was no mortar holding the bricks in place, and they were removed after the Surveyor had gone, to reveal the glass window behind. That was tax evasion, and if you were caught doing it, your window tax was doubled!

Tax evasion is not confined to the "black economy" where payment is in cash and the taxman is never told about it. **In fact, it can be as simple as failing to correct an error in your tax return, once you realise that you have underpaid tax** (or had too much tax repaid to you). This is one reason why a professional adviser will explicitly require your authorisation to be able to correct your tax return if such an error is uncovered: the error itself may have been entirely innocent – which is fine – but failure to remedy it once discovered is another matter entirely.

It is likely that any "tax planning" scheme that relies on HMRC not knowing the full facts about a transaction is in fact an example of tax evasion.

Obviously, none of the strategies described in this guide involve tax evasion in any form, but in one or two cases we shall be pointing out the danger of crossing the line between avoidance and evasion (such as those involving tax "planning" for your home).

HMRC also has a regime for **Managing Serious Defaulters** – where a penalty is incurred for a misdeclaration in a tax return and HMRC determines that the corresponding underpayment of tax has arisen deliberately, then:

- Broadly where the tax deemed at risk was more than £25,000, then HMRC may publish certain of the taxpayer's details as a "Deliberate Defaulter", (so that it may be seen by the general public), and

- The taxpayer may be subjected to enhanced monitoring of their tax affairs for a period of up to 5 years, wherein their tax returns will be carefully scrutinised, and they may need to furnish such further information as HMRC prescribes – and, in some cases, provide financial security to offset the risk of further defaults in future

This may initially look like the regime for Serial Tax Avoiders at 4.7 but there is a key difference: a Serious/Deliberate Defaulter has deliberately underdeclared their tax position, (*evasion*), whereas a Serial Tax Avoider has merely shown a predilection for packaged tax *avoidance* schemes, that have not worked.

4.9 Penalties for "Enablers" and Promoters of Tax Avoidance, etc.

If you think life as a taxpayer is getting rather complicated, rest assured that tax adviser firms do not have it any easier. Finance Act 2017 included provisions that introduced a new **penalty for 'enablers' of tax avoidance schemes** that are considered 'abusive' and are subsequently defeated by HMRC. Enablers are generally professional advisers who design, market or otherwise facilitate tax avoidance. The penalty for the enabler is up to 100% of the fees earned for such work, and applies for arrangements and enabling action commenced on or after 16 November 2017.

Separately, HMRC is continuing to refine its powers for dealing with ***Promoters* Of Tax Avoidance Schemes (POTAS)**, which include:

- HMRC may **demand information** broadly along the same lines as under DOTAS, (4.4), at short notice, rather than wait for the adviser to decide if a Scheme they are selling is notifiable under DOTAS.

- HMRC may issue a "**Stop Notice**" to prevent a firm engaging in any further promotion of a tax avoidance Scheme, subject to certain criteria (such as likelihood the Scheme will fail). HMRC may now publicise where it has issued a Stop Notice; at the time of writing, the government is consulting on making it a criminal offence, if a firm fails to comply with a Stop Notice

- **Conduct Notices and Monitoring Notices**, where HMRC can take steps to dissuade a firm from undertaking certain types of work or activities, to require the firm to disclose that it is being monitored by HMRC, (and HMRC can publicise that firms are the subject of a monitoring notice)

Mandatory Disclosure Rules - As part of an international accord between numerous tax jurisdictions, the government has imposed a new regime that will legally require promoters and advisers to disclose details of certain "arrangements" to HMRC, where those "arrangements" try to use opaque offshore structures in cross-border tax schemes, to hide the true ownership of assets from the tax authorities. HMRC will share such information with other tax authorities where relevant, and *vice versa*.

Failure to Prevent Tax Evasion / Fraud – A corporate criminal offence arises where a firm fails to take reasonable steps to prevent the *facilitation* of tax evasion by its employees or associates, either in the UK or even overseas in some cases; under the draft Economic Crime and Corporate Transparency Bill, some firms may be liable if their employee or agent commits specified categories of fraud, including false accounting, and the organisation did **not** have reasonable fraud-prevention measures in place (regardless of whether the firm knew about the fraud).

This comprises a quick tour of just some of the measures that the government has introduced in the last few years. But it should be emphasised that **the advice that**

follows in the rest of this book is intended to fall squarely in the domain of acceptable tax planning.

5 Key Tax Dates for Your Diary

The UK's tax system is currently based on "Self-Assessment".

5.1 Self-Assessment: The Basics

People who have untaxed income (such as rents from property or income from self-employment), or who have high incomes generally, are sent an annual Self-Assessment Return for each tax year, shortly after the end of that year on 5 April.

If you are in this category, you will already be familiar with the way the system works, and the relevant deadlines for filing your return and paying the tax.

If you do not receive a Self-Assessment return (or "notice to file" each April, however, and you have:

- Started a trade, such as property development
- Started receiving untaxed income, such as rental income from property, or
- Made a capital gain which is not exempt from CGT (and see the new regime for residential property disposals below)

- then it is your responsibility to notify HMRC and to request a Self-Assessment Return.

In most cases, the deadline for this is 5 October after the end of the tax year, so if (say) you first let a property during the year ending 5 April 2023, you must notify HMRC of this by 5 October 2023. (Please see later for issues specific to trading and property development).

Once in the "Self-Assessment" system, you are required to file the return (by 31 October after the end of the tax year if you file a paper return, and 31 January if you do it online) and pay any tax due by 31 January following the end of the tax year – so for 2022/23, the tax (and the return if filed online) will be due on 31 January 2024.

In future years, you will be required to make annual payments on account, on 31 July and on 31 January (again – which can make 31 January very expensive!) – your Self-Assessment Return will explain the details.

There are penalties for failing to notify HMRC of your new source of income, or your capital gains, by the 5 October deadline, so do not delay!

Introductory Example Illustrating Self-Assessment Timings on Commencement

> Davina works (say) as an employed chartered surveyor, and already pays Income Tax through PAYE at the higher rate of 40%. In July 2022, she decided to undertake a project, to buy, develop and sell on a run-down property near where she lives. This is the first time that Davina has done something outside of her paid employment. As this new activity commenced in the 2022/23 tax year, she has until 5 October 2023 to notify HMRC.
>
> Davina sold the developed property in March 2023, making a profit of £30,000. She decides that she has made a decent return on her investment of time and money,

so she will carry on the property development activity. She notifies HMRC that she has a new chargeable income source in April 2023, and HMRC duly sends her a notice to file a 2022/23 tax return.

Davina has until 31 October 2023 to file her 2022/23 tax return on paper, or until 31January 2024 to file online.

If we assume that PAYE has deducted the correct amount of tax from Davina's employment income during the 2022/23 tax year, and requires no further adjustment, then Davina's Self-Assessment Income Tax as a 40% taxpayer bill will be £12,000 (roughly: ignore self-employed NICs for simplicity).

Davina started the self-employed activity in July 2022, and made profits by 5 April 2023 of £30,000, but has not yet paid any Income Tax.

Davina decides to file her tax return online, which means that she will file her first tax return, and make her first payment of Income Tax through Self-Assessment, on or before 31 January 2024.

In her first year, she will have to pay the first £12,000 in full on 31 January, AND make her first 50% Payment on Account for the next tax year – 2023/24 – of £6,000. She will need to make this additional interim payment because she is continuing in self-employment beyond the initial project. (She can, however, apply to reduce her payment on account if she thinks her Self-assessment tax bill will be lower in 2023/24 than in 2022/23. Note that, while Davina has the option to reduce the payment, she does NOT have to pay more than 50% of the previous year's liability, if she thinks her profits may rise).

Davina will therefore have to pay £18,000 on 31 January 2024. This is a substantial amount, but note that Davina will have been in business for more than 18 months by this date.

She will also have to pay £6,000, (a further 50% of the previous year's bill), on account of her anticipated 2023/24 Self-Assessment liability, by 31 July 2024 (again, Davina could reduce her interim payments for 2023/24 if she thought that her self-employed profits would fall, and her eventual tax bill would be lower than for 2022/23).

Let's assume that Davina makes a net taxable profit of £30,000 in the 2023/24 tax year – the same as for 2022/23. She has therefore paid all of the tax due already, in her 2 interim payments of £6,000, being part of the £18,000 paid on 31 January 2024 and the payment of £6,000 on 31 July 2024.

Davina's Balancing Payment for 2023/24 – due 31 January 2025 – will therefore be £nil. She will, however, have to make her first Payment on Account for 2024/25, which will be based on 50% of the previous year's liability.

If Davina continues to make £30,000 taxable profits from self-employment annually then, all other things remaining equal, she will continue to owe (roughly) £12,000 through Self-Assessment, making payments of £6,000 each on 31 January and 31 July.

There is a substantial "catch-up charge" when the first Self-Assessment payment is required but, provided profits remain flat, the tax payments themselves will level off.

Given that Davina managed to make £30,000 in taxable profits in just 9 months in her first period of self-employment, we might expect her to make higher profits in her first full year – and, potentially, to make higher profits as she gains experience and her self-employed business grows. Under the regime as it currently stands, there is an effective lag until 31 January the following calendar year, to return and pay for those higher profits, and start making correspondingly higher Payments on Account, etc., etc.

This is a simple example. Complicating factors include:

- National Insurance Contributions (as noted above)
- Use (or not) of Capital Allowances: this is a separate regime that gives tax relief for expenditure on qualifying capital assets – from office furniture to tools, to vans.
- Adoption of the traditional "accruals basis" of accounting when preparing the accounts, or "cash accounting" instead.
- Valuation of closing stocks and work-in-progress, depending on the accounting basis adopted.

All of these issues – and more – will be covered in further detail, in Chapters 7 – 11 inclusive.

5.2 New Regime for CGT Payments on Account for Residential Property Disposals

With the 2019 Finance Act, the government introduced a new regime for making CGT payments on account, for disposals of residential property. **Taxpayers will have to notify HMRC *and* make a payment on account of the CGT estimated to be due, within 60 days of completion, for sales (or other chargeable disposals) of residential property that complete on or after 27 October 2021** (prior to that, the window had been just 30 days since the introduction of the regime in April 2020).

This measure is simply designed to improve the Crown's cashflow, to the significant inconvenience of everybody else involved. This new regime is in addition to a taxpayer's existing Self Assessment obligations and such disposals will still need to be included in their Self Assessment tax returns as well (although people will no longer have to enter the Self Assessment regime just to file a "one-off" tax return to cover a capital gain on a residential property disposal).

Practically speaking, the vast majority will still have to estimate the CGT due for the purposes of the 60-day payment on account, and then re-calculate the actual liability once the tax year is complete and other income, gains and losses can be included and/or claimed as appropriate, as part of their ongoing Self-Assessment return cycle.

From the perspective of property businesses, note:

- A property developer selling a property that was acquired and developed for sale at a profit will not be affected because that is a trading asset – stock – rather than a fixed asset subject to a capital gain (but see 7.11 below for property originally acquired as an investment)

- UK-resident companies are unaffected by the new regime because they do not pay CGT through Self-Assessment, but Corporation Tax on capital gains instead

- Where a property developer, etc., *does* sell a residential property either personally or out of the fixed/investment assets of his or her unincorporated business, (including partnerships), then the new regime *will* apply and a notification and provisional payment of CGT will be required – but only if CGT is actually expected to be due (so not if reliefs, etc., should be sufficient fully to offset the capital gain).

- For those individuals who are resident in the UK for tax purposes, the regime applies only to UK residential property on which CGT is estimated to be due, but for persons who are **not** resident in the UK for tax purposes, the regime extends to cover *any* disposals of *any* UK land or buildings, including commercial property, and regardless of whether or not tax is actually due on the disposal. It also applies in some cases even to disposals of shares in UK-resident companies that are effectively owned by overseas / non-resident parties, and are UK "property-rich" – the companies' worth derives predominantly from UK land assets – in other words, it can catch scenarios where the shares in the company that owns UK land (or property) are sold or otherwise disposed of, not the UK land itself.

- In particular, note that a gift or similar transfer is still generally chargeable to CGT – HMRC still wants its slice even if you're happy to forego your proceeds – unless it is a disposal to one's spouse or civil partner, or a special category of asset (such as cars, or certain qualifying business asset, where the gain on the gift can be postponed if not extinguished – see 11.7).

5.3 Making Tax Digital (MTD)

This is a new regime, set to revolutionise how businesses keep their financial records and "file their taxes":

- **Businesses will be obliged to keep their accounting records digitally, rather than on paper.**

- **They will also have to make online returns of income and expenditure on a quarterly basis.**

Essentially, only certain "HMRC-approved" software packages may be used, since HMRC sets the criteria for compliance. (People can use spreadsheets as part of their accounting systems, but as those spreadsheets must be able to "talk" to HMRC's software, their facility and flexibility is likely to be significantly curtailed).

In time, MTD will likely outgrow the Self-Assessment framework into which it now slots. HMRC certainly anticipate that it will generate significantly higher tax revenues as businesses are forced, in HMRC's eyes, to become more compliant.

Timetable for Implementation

- Businesses (including landlords and property developers) with VAT-taxable turnovers in excess of the VAT registration threshold (currently £85,000) had to move to the new digital regime from April 2019. In other words, those businesses that have to be VAT-registered were obliged to operate MTD (but only for VAT purposes) from April 2019.

- From April 2022, all VAT-registered businesses – regardless of turnover – were required to adopt MTD – digital record-keeping and online submission of returns, for VAT purposes.

- **MTD for Income Tax Self-Assessment is intended to apply basically to all unincorporated businesses – including property businesses.** However, HMRC has struggled for years to implement the regime because it has repeatedly failed to acknowledge the huge complexity and disruption that will occur. As of December 2022, the latest schedule is as follows:

  - MTD (Income Tax) for sole traders and landlords with aggregate business income **greater than** £50,000pa will be mandated from April 2026
  - MTD (Income Tax) for sole traders and landlords with aggregate business income **greater than** £30,000pa will be mandated from April 2027
  - MTD (Income Tax) for sole traders and landlords with aggregate business income **lower than** £30,000pa will be subject to further review, to inform the approach of any further roll-out after April 2027
  - MTD (Income Tax) for partnerships is "to be advised"

  The new timetable has been drawn up to give the smallest businesses more time to prepare.

- HMRC has **not** yet fixed a date for MTD for Corporation Tax but this is likely to follow April 2026 (although the timetable may yet slip further).

Businesses with annual turnover below £10,000 will **not** have to comply with MTD for Income Tax (unless they want to). But note that for individuals, this threshold applies to annual income aggregated across all of their businesses, and the exception will therefore apply in very limited circumstances.

Basically, the only parties driving this forwards are HMRC and book-keeping software companies.

It seems likely that many businesses will quite wrongly assume that, so long as they are able to file their quarterly returns ("updates") to HMRC online, then they will have done enough to comply with MTD. **This is absolutely incorrect.**

The biggest issue behind MTD is the requirement to keep financial records digitally, so as to ensure that financial information is entered only once, and that this stored information is submitted to HMRC without further manual intervention.

Businesses themselves, and their advisers, are hugely concerned about the additional cost and time involved. Property development businesses often do not need to register for VAT but sometimes they will do so voluntarily, so as to be able to reclaim VAT on their costs (although strictly, notification is mandatory even if taxable supplies are zero-rated). Other property developers *are* obliged to register for VAT, depending on the nature of the work that they do. All but the smallest businesses will need to keep an eye on the MTD regime as the story unfolds – and will do well to ensure that their book-keeping software, etc., is capable of being made MTD-compliant.

6 Anti-Avoidance Legislation – "Transactions in UK Land"

We shall shortly be looking at the taxation of property developers, but before we do, we need to consider this piece of anti-avoidance legislation, which can cause problems for the owners of investment properties or indeed other land (or buildings) when they sell it – not least because many people have never heard of it!

The "Transactions in UK Land" regime has been around for many years, but was overhauled in the 2016 Finance Act. Any pretence at simplification has been dispensed with: it has now been liberally spread amongst 2 Income Tax Acts and 2 Corporation Tax Acts.

What the regime does is to treat certain transactions in land as if they produced trading income rather than capital gains – and this can be expensive! In many cases, property developers are already trading, so this is unlikely to affect most of their projects. But the regime will bite if a capital asset is developed with a profit motive on sale: you might *think* you are merely enhancing a capital asset to improve its marketability for CGT purposes, but this regime says otherwise. Typically, it is property *investors* who have most to lose from the Transactions in Land provisions, since their rental properties are generally held as capital assets, and may well be developed prior to eventual sale. But property developers may also hold land or buildings as capital assets and need to consider how Transactions in Land may affect them.

"A slice of the action" and "Transactions in Land"

Norman has owned three buy to let properties on adjacent plots since March 2000 – they cost him a total of £100,000.

He is thinking of selling them, and has had a valuation of £450,000 for the three properties from an estate agent. He starts to consult with an architect on a number of possible planning applications.

In 2023, he is approached by a developer, who is confident he can get planning permission to build a new apartment block on the land.

She offers Norman a deal:

- £400,000 up front when Norman sells her the properties
- £50,000 when full planning permission for the development is achieved
- A "slice of the action", in the form of 20% of the profit on the development itself (the developer reckons Norman's 20% could be worth up to £200,000)

This "slice of the action" will be payable one year after the initial payment.

Norman accepts the deal.

He knows a bit about Capital Gains Tax, including the way "contingent consideration" (the payment on getting planning permission) and "unascertainable future consideration" (the "slice of the action") are taxed, and so he *expects* that he will be taxed as follows:

"The £400,000 and the £50,000, together with the present value of the future right to up to £200,000 will be added together, and treated as the sale price – if I assume that the present value of the 20% "slice of the action" is agreed as £150,000, the total sale price will be £600,000. With a base cost of £100,000, I will make a gain of £500,000, taxable at 28%."*

(Norman also figures that, if he eventually gets more than the £150,000 that his "slice of the action" was valued at, he will also pay CGT on that amount, again at 28% - for convenience of calculation).

Unfortunately, Norman will be caught by the Transactions in Land rules, because his "slice of the action" is actually giving him a chance to participate in the profits of a trading transaction (the development and sale of the apartment block), and this is therefore taxable as income, rather than as a capital gain.

* **Note** while the Chancellor announced in the March 2016 Budget that CGT rates would generally fall to 10% and 20% (the latter for higher rate taxpayers), the previous, more punitive rates of 18% and 28% remain for residential property gains – and in this context, this includes "...land that has, **at any time in the person's ownership**, consisted of or included a dwelling", so Norman will be caught.

Although the initial £450,000 will still be taxed as a capital gain, anything Norman gets under his "slice of the action" of the developer's profit on sale, will be taxed as income under the Transactions in Land rules.

Let us assume that Norman's "slice of the action" actually produces the £200,000 the developer had predicted, and that Norman is already a higher rate taxpayer, so all taxable capital gains will be at 28%.

If everything were treated as a capital gain, as Norman initially hoped:

		Tax payable
Initial proceeds:		
Lump sum	400,000	
Payment on successful planning permission	50,000	
Current value of contingent payment	150,000	
Total proceeds	600,000	
Deduct: cost of properties	(100,000)	
Net gain:	500,000	

Less Annual Exempt Amount (2023/24)	(6,000)	
Taxable	494,000	
CGT @ 28% (already pays income tax @ 40%)		138,320
Gain in later tax year on "Slice of the action"		
Actual proceeds in later year	200,000	
Less: original estimate in 2023/24	(150,000)	
Gain taxable in later year	50,000	
Annual exempt amount then (say)	(3,000)	
Taxable	47,000	
CGT @ 28%		13,160
Total CGT due		**147,112**

Because of the Transactions in Land rules, the tax treatment is actually very different:

		Tax payable
Initial proceeds:		
Lump sum	400,000	
Payment on successful planning permission	50,000	
Slice of the action ignored for CGT – it is actually taxable as income	-	
Total proceeds	450,000	
Deduct: cost of properties	(100,000)	
Net gain:	350,000	
Less Annual Exempt Amount (2023/24)	(6,000)	

Taxable	344,000	
CGT @ 28% (already pays income tax @40%)		96,320
Slice of the action (treated as income)	200,000	
Income tax @ 40/45% (say)		90,000
Total tax due		**186,320**

Norman ends up paying a lot more tax – almost £40,000 more – through the "Transactions in Land" route, which he cannot avoid, because his "slice of the action" reward is deemed to be sharing in the property developer's profits – and is caught for Income Tax on that proportion of the overall proceeds he gets for the deal. This, of course, because Income Tax rates as high as 45% work out more expensive than even the punitive 28% rate for capital gains on residential property disposals. In some cases, trading NICs can be due, to further increase the charge due on the development-for-profit activity.

Norman will obviously prefer as much as possible to be taxed as a capital gain – essentially the "up-front" pre-development payment. But it is also a question of how much the developer is prepared to risk – or can afford to commit so early – before the developer sees any return of his or her own.

Note that developing an investment property is NOT automatically caught if the aim of the development is to benefit from an improved investment property, rather than for resale at a profit. In other words, it is less likely that the regime will apply, if the land or property is enhanced but then retained as a fixed asset investment for an appreciable period, rather than being sold on immediately that the development work has finished.

Caution: The Transactions in Land regime is very complicated, and we have simplified the way it works for the purposes of this Case Study, which is intended simply to illustrate the sort of circumstances that can be caught.

Now the good news:

- The rules cannot apply to a gain on the disposal of one's main residence, even if it is caught by the "intention to realise a gain" rules – see Chapters 8 & 9 below.

  Mr Green, in 8.3 below, might have a problem, however, if he were given a "slice of the action" on the sale of part of his garden, because as we shall see, that did not qualify for the main residence exemption.

- In a case where you are not certain if you will be caught by the Transactions in Land rules, it is possible to get a "clearance" from HMRC before you agree to the deal.

Provided you give them the full facts, if they then agree *not* to apply the Transactions in Land rules, they cannot change their minds later.

"Slice of the action" deals are not the only type of transaction that can be caught by these rules, but they are by far the commonest example of how people can be caught out, without either realising it, or having intended to avoid tax.

The "Transactions in Land" regime (strictly, "Profits from Trading in and Developing UK Land", although most will recognise the regime by its old nickname) is definitely a job for a tax expert, and you should consult your tax adviser about it if:

- You are offered a "slice of the action" deal for the sale of land, or
- You are contemplating the development of land originally held as an investment, or a fixed or capital asset of the business, and you do NOT have a fixed intention to retain the property as an investment for the long term afterwards.
- You are offered any deal involving the sale of land that seems rather complicated – such as staged payments, or deferred, progress or milestone payments

7 Trading in Property

If you buy a property with the intention of selling it on at a profit in the short term, then even if you receive some rental income from it while you own it, you are **trading** and your profit from selling the property will be charged to Income Tax – and to National Insurance Contributions (NICs).

In this section of the guide, we shall look at the tax treatment of:

- "Turnarounds" where a property is bought (perhaps at an auction) and sold at a profit with little or no work done on it
- "Refurbs" where a property is bought, significantly altered (perhaps by being converted into flats, or by being extensively renovated), and then sold at a profit
- "New builds", where a new property is built and sold.

7.1 Notifying HMRC you have Started Trading

Notification:
When you begin to trade, you should notify HMRC promptly – and certainly by 5 October of the tax year following commencement. If you do not do so, there are potentially quite severe penalties for longer delays (see also 5.1).

The simplest way to register is to visit the "Self-Assessment" page on HMRC's part of the GOV.UK website.

7.2 National Insurance (NI) Contributions (and Levies)

A trader is liable to pay "Class 4" NIC on his profits.

2023/24 Self-Employed ("Class 4") NI Rates	
First £12,570	NIL
Next £37,700	9.00%
Any additional profits over £50,270	2.00%

Readers will recall that the government announced a new "Health and Social Care Levy" in early September 2021, that was supposed to add 1.25% - broadly as an addition to NICs. 2022 saw numerous last-minute tweaks to the NICs regime until the new Levy was formally **abandoned,** before it had even properly begun, in late 2022.

It did, however, leave two more lasting changes:

1. In his 2022 Spring Statement, the Chancellor announced his intention to align the Lower Profits Limit – the threshold at which Class 4 NICs start to become payable – with the Income Tax Personal Allowance (currently £12,570). This is now reflected in the 2023/24 threshold above, and represents a significant increase on previous years.

2. In order that people receiving dividends did not feel left out by the new Levy, Finance Act 2022 increased dividend tax rates by 1.25% across all bands from April 2022 (save for the Nil% band itself); mysteriously, that 1.25% hike has remained, even though the Levy itself has been abolished. Some advisers are beginning to realise that dividends can now in some cases be more expensive than simple salary or bonus – for more on this, see another of our books "**How to Use Companies to Reduce Property Taxes**", or my Business Tax Insider article "**The Director's Loan Account: A Cheap Source of Income**?"

In addition to Class 4 NIC, you are also required to pay "Class 2" NIC, calculated at a rate of £3.45 per week. By default, it is collected alongside Class 4 NIC and income tax on your self-assessment return.

Class 2 NICs are important because they are the self-employed component of NICs that 'earns' a credit for State Pension and, while Class 4 NICs were supposed to take over that role, *they* are not triggered until earnings reach £12,570pa, leaving 'lower' earners able to garner a State Pension record only by paying voluntary Class 3 NICs which are much more expensive at £17.45 a week.

However, as part of the overhaul of NICs introduced in the 2022 Spring Statement, the Chancellor announced that the government would align the threshold at which Class 2 NICs start to be payable alongside that for Class 4 NICs – i.e., £12,570 in 2023/24 and then alongside the Personal Allowance of £12,570 thereafter – but that self-employed profits at a minimum threshold of £6,725pa would nevertheless be sufficient to 'earn' the State Pension credit, even while profits were too low to trigger actual payment of Class 2 NICs. In the longer term, it seems very likely that Class 2 NICs and Class 4 NICs will be merged.

If you ring the Income Tax Helpline, (**0300 200 3500**), you should be sent full details of all of this.

If you are also an employee, it may be possible to **reduce** your Class 4 NIC liability.

For example, if you are already paying the maximum employee NI contributions through PAYE on your salary, (which you will be if your earnings exceed £50,270 in 2023/24), then your Class 4 NICs will be limited to just 2.0% of profits over the Lower Profits Limit (£12,570 in 2023/24). If your NIC'able earnings from employment are less than the Upper Earnings Limit of £50,270, then a proportion of your self-employed earnings will be exposed to the 9% "full" rate, etc.

7.3 Income Tax and NIC for the Property Developer

The following Case Study illustrates how Income Tax and NIC are charged on a property developer's profits:

Charging of Income Tax and NIC

Simone sets herself up as a property developer, buying a rundown house on 6 April 2023 for £70,000. She spends £30,000 on renovation work, and sells the house on 1st March 2024 for £160,000.

She has made a trading profit of £60,000. Assuming she has no other income for 2023/24, her profit will be taxed as follows:

Income Tax		**Payable**
Profit for 2023/24	60,000	
Less personal allowance	(12,570)	Nil
Taxable	47,430	
Taxed at 20%	37,700	7,540
Balance taxed at 40%	9,730	3,892
National Insurance Class 4	60,000	
Lower Profits Limit	(12,570)	
	47,430	
Taxed at main rate of 9.0%	37,700	3,393
Chargeable above Upper Profits Level (2.0%)	9,730	195
Add: Class 2 NIC @ £3.45/wk		179
Total tax and NIC payable 31 January 2024		**15,199**

7.4 New £1,000 Allowances – Guard Your Losses

The Finance (No.2) Act 2017 included two new Allowances, each of £1,000. From 2017/18 onwards, the Trading Allowance covers trading and casual income, while the Property Allowance covers income from letting, for example from charging other people for parking their car on one's drive during the working day. The Allowances are aimed at removing very modest income sources from the tax regime.

As regards the Trading Allowance, where **gross income** (not net profit!) from trading or casual income is less than £1,000 in the tax year, then any income and expenses are simply ignored, leaving the taxable amount at £nil.

Where gross income exceeds £1,000 then it is possible to claim the £1,000 Allowance instead of actual expenses – useful if income is a little above £1,000, and actual expenses are minimal.

The same approach applies to the Property Allowance in relation to income from property.

Property developers are **un**likely to benefit from the Trading Allowance: their incomes and expenses are likely to be well in excess of £1,000. If, however, a property developer were to have only minimal income in a year but (say) substantial expenses, note that it is technically possible to forfeit your losses where income is less than £1,000, since the Allowance will be granted automatically, and any expenses ignored – even if they result in net losses. It is, however, possible to elect to disapply the regime, so as to claim your losses in full.

There are similar rules for the Property Allowance; neither Allowance may be claimed against income that is, or could be, subject to Rent a Room relief (see **8.9**).

7.5 Property Development and Limited Companies

In some cases, it may be advantageous to use a limited company for your property development trade. This is because a company starts paying Corporation Tax at only 19% on its profits – so on a profit of £60,000 like Simone's above, the corporation tax would be only £12,150. (Note: the Chancellor announced in the 2021 Budget that the main rate of Corporation Tax would increase to 25% from 1 April 2023, but the first £50,000 of company profits is usually still taxed at only 19%, as before).

A comparison between running your development business self-employed *versus* through a company is not as simple as this, however: if you want to extract the cash from the company for your personal use, then there may be additional tax costs. Even so, if Simone were to run her property development business through a company instead of personally, she could save almost £2,500 in overall tax and NICs costs in 2023/24 alone.

The decision whether to use a company or not is not straight forward – see our guide **"How to Use Companies to Reduce Property Taxes"**, available from www.property-tax-portal.co.uk.

7.6 Accounts and Records

It is essential to set up a good record-keeping system to keep track of your income and outgoings, and to keep those records safely – this is equally true of rental income, of course, but in the case of trading records, you are required to keep the records until the fifth anniversary of the 31 January after the end of the tax year – so for 2023/24, the records must be kept until at least 31 January 2030. See also Making Tax Digital in Chapter 5 about digital record-keeping requirements, as will soon apply in many cases.

A trader's accounts are generally prepared on the "accruals" basis – See 10.4. Historically, traders have been able to choose whatever year-end or accounting date they like, for their accounts and chargeable periods. However, the government announced in the Autumn 2021 Budget that ALL businesses must now adopt the tax year end basis, starting April 2024.

Established trading businesses that have not already adopted the end of the tax year as their accounting reference date will have some significant transitional adjustments to make in 2023/24. This wholescale change to the taxation of trading individuals and partnerships has been introduced to make things easier for HMRC, as part of its drive towards Making Tax Digital.

There remains a little flexibility in choice of accounting date for tax purposes: anywhere between 31 March and 5 April is still permissible, but the choice of accounting date will no longer make any real difference to the taxation of profits for the year.

7.7 The Construction Industry Scheme ("CIS")

If you engage in "property development", you will be required to register for and operate this scheme.

It does not normally apply to property investors (such as Buy to Let landlords), and if you really only do minimal refurbishment on your "turnarounds" you MAY be able to justify not joining it, but **if you do "refurbs", or if you engage in property development, you will be a "property developer" for the purposes of the CIS, and you must register as a "contractor".**

What do these words mean?

A "property developer" could be an individual, a partnership, or a limited company. The key is, do they earn their profits by doing building work – either by new builds which they then sell, or by buying an existing property, and improving it, and then selling it on? If so, then they are a property developer.

A **"contractor"** is a person – including a company – whose business involves using (contracting) **other** people's labour to carry out building work. Almost all "property developers" use the services of independent bricklayers, carpenters, painters, electricians, plasterers, and so on, so almost all developers will be "contractors" when doing so.

"Buy to Let" investors will generally **not** be "property developers" or "contractors" because, while they may use the same tradesmen to do work on their properties, they make their income from renting them out, not from selling them – they are investors, not traders. If they spend more than £3million in any 12-month period on "construction operations", however, then they will be pushed into the scheme as a "**deemed contractor**". Likewise, if they undertake a substantial development project – even for letting purposes – HMRC may argue that they are temporarily "caught" by the regime.

(A "deemed contractor" is basically a person whose main activity is **not** construction work, such as a landlord or retailer, but whose overall business activity involves sufficient construction operations to trip the £3million rolling 12-month threshold. The threshold worked a little differently, prior to April 2021. Unfortunately, HMRC does not even stick to this rule, particularly when it comes to landlords, and will often try to argue that their business includes "construction operations" during a major construction project, and has temporarily become a mainstream contractor, therefore bypassing the deemed contractor threshold.)

The "Construction Industry Scheme" imposes very onerous duties on "contractors" and "subcontractors". In order to understand why the scheme is as it is, we need to look at its history...

Back in the 1960s, the construction industry in the UK was notorious for widespread tax evasion. Workers on building sites, who told the foreman their names were "Michael Mouse", or "Roy Rogers", got paid in cash, and had never seen a tax return in their lives. When the Tax Inspector attempted to trace them, to his or her surprise, there was no Mr Mouse at the given address – and often the address was false as well.

There were two basic problems:

- Some of the "Mickey Mice" were really employees of the building contractor, and should have had PAYE applied to their wages through payroll

- The rest of them, though genuinely self-employed, did not declare their income and pay tax and NICs on it through their own tax returns, as they should have done

Against this background, the "Construction Industry Scheme" ("**CIS**") was first introduced in 1970. Since then, it has been much modified – with a major "reform" in 1999, and more major changes taking place in April 2007. The basic concept of the scheme remains the same, however.

The CIS is based on HMRC's distrust of everyone involved in the construction industry. It assumes that if builders are allowed to conduct their tax affairs like any other business in the land, they will lie, cheat and basically evade their tax.

The Construction Industry Scheme

Jackie owns a plot of land with planning permission to build a house on it. She decides she will build a house and sell it. She knows she will occasionally need specialists to do some of the work.

At this point, Jackie has decided to trade as a property developer – a speculative builder, in fact – so she is now a "contractor" for CIS purposes. Jackie must immediately register with HMRC as a "contractor". She is obliged to read through many pages of guidance on how to operate the scheme as an unpaid tax collector.

Jackie talks to Bob (the builder), and they agree a price for Bob and his workforce to build the house. It is agreed that Jackie will pay Bob £5,000 when his men start work.

Jackie must contact HMRC (online) to verify if Bob is registered as a subcontractor.

HMRC confirms Bob is registered for "Gross Payment".

Jackie can pay Bob without deducting tax.

Jackie has also asked an electrician, Michael Faraday, to do the wiring on the new house. Before paying him, she contacts HMRC, who tell her that Michael is registered for "Net Payment".

Jackie must deduct 20% tax from payments to Michael in relation to his construction services – generally, the invoice net of materials costs. If Michael had not been registered at all, (basically, if HMRC said they had never heard of Mr. Michael Faraday), then the tax to deduct would have been 30%.

Once a month, Jackie must send the tax she has deducted to HMRC, together with a return of payments made, signed to certify that she has operated the scheme correctly. This must be done within 14 days of the end of the month (but Jackie must remember that a CIS month ends on the 5th day of the following month, so in fact she has until 19 July to send in her deductions for June). ***This regime must still be followed even when no CIS payments are made that month****, although it is possible to make a Scheme temporarily 'dormant'.*

That was a VERY abbreviated version of how the scheme works – the reality is more complicated and difficult to comply with.

7.8 Why Bother with the CIS?

The short answer is that there are penalties if you don't!

If Jackie failed to register as a contractor, or failed to deduct tax from payments to Michael, she could be liable for:

- Penalties of up to £900 for **each** late monthly return she makes (it could be more in cases where the CIS tax is high enough – and potentially an extra £3,000 or more per return, if the return is more than 12 months late, depending on whether or not HMRC decides the failure to file on time was deliberate)
- Unless Jackie can satisfy HMRC that Michael has paid his tax himself, Jackie can be liable for the 20% tax that Jackie *should* have deducted from the payments she made to Michael
- Few people set out to be "more than 12 months late" to file one or more CIS returns. But if you have been trading as a property developer for (say) three or four years, but never registered for CIS, then you will have **dozens** of returns that are more than a year late.

If you are trading as a property developer, building (or buying and improving) properties for sale, you are automatically a "Mainstream Contractor" and liable to operate the CIS. There is no lower limit below which you do not have to operate this scheme.

One of the many unjust features of the CIS regime is that there are probably a lot of small-scale property developers out there who do not know they should be operating the scheme.

Those who *do* comply with the scheme are at a disadvantage, because many small "domestic"-sized building firms simply will not work for a CIS-registered "contractor" due to the bureaucratic and cashflow implications; meanwhile, builders who work only on people's own homes, with the homeowner as the direct client, are **not** required to be in the CIS.

To find out more about the CIS, visit HMRC's website and look for "CIS" – or speak to your Tax Adviser. See also 7.20 Employed or Self-Employed?

7.9 VAT

This is unlikely to be an issue for the typical buy to let landlord, as the letting of almost all residential property is an exempt supply, so he or she cannot register for VAT, but also cannot claim back any of the input VAT on expenses. For the "turnaround" or the "refurb" property business, the purchase and sale of an existing property is **usually** an exempt supply as well, so again it will not be possible to recover the VAT.

But it is possible still to reduce your VAT costs – for example, if a property has been vacant for over two years, or if you buy it and then change the number of dwellings it contains (for example by converting it into flats, or by knocking two flats into one), then although the *sale* of the building may still be exempt, any VAT-registered contractor you use may be able to charge you a reduced rate of 5% VAT on their invoices, including the cost of most materials (the normal rate of VAT is currently 20%). **So, for example, the cost of a standard £1,200 (VAT-inclusive) invoice to you as a non-VAT-registered business would fall to £1,050, where the reduced rate applies instead, across the whole invoice.**

A **commercial property** landlord may decide to register for VAT so that he (or she) can recover the VAT on any expenses. If he wants to do this, he will usually have to "opt to tax" the rents he charges on that property. Whether he decides to do this or not may well depend on the sort of tenants he has – if they are themselves fully taxable for VAT purposes (as most businesses are), they will be quite happy, as they will be able to recover all of the VAT on their own rental costs.

If, however, the tenants are 'small' traders who trade below the threshold for VAT registration and do not want to register voluntarily, or if they are exempt or partially exempt (as are most financial businesses and insurance companies), they will be very unenthusiastic about paying any VAT on the rent that they cannot then fully recover.

A property developer doing only residential new-builds may well *want* to register for VAT, because when he or she sells the completed building, it will be "zero rated" (**not** exempt, but a VAT rate of 0%) so he will then be able to recover most of his VAT without having to charge any tangible VAT to the purchaser.

Typically, the problems arise when the business engages in a mixture of these activities – for example, if it does new-builds and refurbs, then some of its sales will be exempt from VAT (i.e., most refurbs), and some will be zero rated (sales of new-builds). This will mean that the business is "partially exempt", which in turn can lead to problems in recovering the VAT on costs that cannot be specifically attributed to specific sales (such as, dare I say it, fees from the business' Tax Adviser!).

The above is a very brief summary of the main VAT issues that may arise for a trader involved with property.

Caution: **The VAT treatment of land and buildings is one of the most complicated aspects of VAT.** If you are planning to engage in property development or refurbishment/conversions to let out, you should take advice from a suitably qualified Tax Adviser. If you are buying or selling commercial property, then you should speak to a Tax Adviser. See also the new VAT Reverse Charge on Construction Services at 4.2.3.

7.10 Property Developers and Trading Stock

As a trader in property, the land or properties you buy for development and/or resale are your **trading stock** or work-in-progress. At the end of each year, you include the cost of any stock you have not sold in your balance sheet, and it becomes your "opening stock" for your next year of trading. This means that you do not get a tax deduction for your trading stock until you sell it:

Trading Stock

Letitia begins trading as a property developer. In her first year she buys two plots of land, Plot A and Plot B, for £10,000 each.

At the end of the year, she has spent £40,000 on constructing a house on Plot A, and £30,000 on constructing a house on Plot B. She has not sold either house.

Her "Closing Stock and Work-in-Progress" for Year 1 will be:

Plot A (initial cost + construction to date)	£50,000
Plot B (initial cost + construction to date)	£40,000
Total Stock (Carried Forwards)	£90,000

During Year 2, she spends another £10,000 on Plot A, finishing the house, which she sells for £100,000. She spends another £30,000 on Plot B, but does not sell it.

For Year 2, her stock will be:

Opening Stock (Brought Forwards from Year 1)	£90,000	
Add: Expenditure in year	£40,000	
Deduct: Cost of Plot A Sold	(£60,000)	
Closing Stock Carried Forwards (Plot B)	£70,000	

The £60,000 expenditure on Plot A is taken from Stock and set against the £100,000 sale proceeds to arrive at the profit of £40,000 on that sale. Note that closing stock equates to the cost to date in Plot B, which has not yet been sold.

This is a simplified version of how trading stock works, but the important point is that the cost of your stock is carried forward until you sell it. If you are considering substantial property development projects – and particularly those that may take several years/accounting periods to complete – you should take expert advice on how closing stock, work-in-progress and "long term contracts" should be valued.

Note that "closing stock", etc., is an accounting adjustment required when using traditional bases of accounting, not the simple "cash basis". The majority of trading property developers will **not** want to adopt the cash basis, despite its vaunted simplicity, because **the cash basis for <u>traders</u> permits only a measly £500 for annual finance costs**. See also 7.13 & 10.4,10.5 for more on how the cash basis works as a concept – but note that for Buy-to-Let businesses, which are not trading businesses, there is no £500 ceiling for annual finance costs (although there are other constraints).

7.11 Property Not Originally Acquired as Trading Stock

In most cases, it will be clear that a property developer is trading – he or she buys bare land or a building, builds on the land or improves the building, and then sells it.

The situation is not so clear-cut if the land or building in question was not acquired as trading stock, such as where it was inherited, or where a buy to let investor decides to develop and sell a property he has owned and rented out for some time.

Land Not Acquired as Trading Stock

Rebecca inherited a two-acre field from her aunt in 2002. It was valued at £70,000, as at the time there was no prospect of getting planning permission for it.

She used the field to graze her horse until 2023, when it became apparent that it might now be possible to get planning permission for four houses. The land becomes much more valuable – say £500,000.

- If Rebecca simply gets outline planning permission and sells the land, she will realise a capital gain – likely in this case to be £430,000, or potentially more, if she is able to sell with planning permission.

- If she sells the land to a developer on a "slice of the action" deal, she will make a capital gain, though she may have problems with the "Transactions in Land" regime (see 4.2.4 above).

- If she decides to do the development herself, hiring architects, builders, and so on to construct the houses, and sells them, the position is more complicated: is she trading, or merely enhancing a capital asset?

  Thanks to the Transactions in Land approach, the most likely interpretation of the facts will be that at the point that she decided to go ahead with the development herself and to make a profit, she "appropriated" the land as trading stock.

If you "appropriate" a capital asset you own to trading stock, you are treated as if you had disposed of it for CGT purposes at its market value, and in your trading accounts you treat it as if you had bought it at the same value.

If you wish, you can elect to "hold over" the capital gain you just made on the land by "appropriating" it, so that you do not pay CGT, but the whole profit (including the gain you have just elected to hold over) is taxed as trading profits when you sell the land/property.

It may be to your advantage <u>not</u> to do this, however, despite the apparent cashflow benefit, as CGT is charged at up to 28%, (for residential property), whereas your trading profits will be taxed at up to 45%, potentially plus NIC.

Essentially, Rebecca has a choice if she decides to develop her land herself:

1. Stand a 20% CGT charge on the notional capital gain when she disposes of her investment land to herself; (note that in this case the land has no dwelling on it so is taxable at only 20% maximum); albeit she may not have the funds to pay any tax – she hasn't really sold anything; or,

2. She can make the election to postpone the capital gain into the eventual sale of the development – potentially paying at (45% + 2% NICs) = 47% (but at least she will have some proceeds from selling the development to pay her tax bill!). The difference is likely to be based on that gain of £430,000 and whether it is taxable to CGT 'early' at 20%, or taxable later as trading income, at 45% or 47% (although the value may shift on achieving planning permission).

The election also used to be potentially beneficial where, if Rebecca's land had *lost* value prior to development, so she was looking at a capital loss, then she could make the election and effectively convert that into an Income Tax loss, by reducing her profits from the development stage. Unfortunately, the government deemed this was "unfair" to HMRC, so elections will now be permitted only when the land is standing at a gain (for appropriations on or after 8 March 2017)

Now, let's consider a slightly different scenario.

Rebecca's brother Tom inherited a rundown old house from another aunt. He decided to sell it quite quickly, but first he spent some money on refurbishing and improving it.

Whether Tom is trading or not is a more difficult question – arguably, he is not changing the nature of the asset he inherited (a house) but merely taking steps to get the best price for it. However, it could be argued that the "Transactions in Land" rules have again been triggered, if HMRC feels that he has "developed" the property.

Alternatively, he could formally "appropriate" the house to a new trade of property development. Note that, if the value of the property has risen from his inheriting the property to when he moves it to trading stock then he will have made a gain on residential property – and be liable both to the higher rates of CGT that apply for residential property, **and** to the 60-day notification and payment on account regime as set out in 5.2 above (assuming the gain exceeds his available CGT Annual Exemption, and he therefore has a taxable gain to report).

Why would he want to do this? If he were to stick with the capital gains route, he would have his annual exempt amount of £6,000 to deduct from the gain made on eventual sale, whereas if he were to plump for trading, he would be liable to Income Tax on the profit, AND to NICs) – at potentially a much higher overall rate.

There are a couple of reasons why he might make the choice to trade:

- **Certainty** – the whole issue of when you start trading with property like this is a "grey area", but if you deliberately "appropriate" the asset to trading stock, HMRC will find it very difficult to argue that you have not done this
- **Interest on loans** – if Tom had to borrow money to pay for the improvements, he would not get relief for the interest he paid if the property were sold for a capital gain, whereas for a property developer, the interest would be allowable as a deduction from trading profits

There is a third possible reason for this "appropriation" – it is sometimes better to trade as a property developer through a limited company, and "appropriating" an asset to trading stock can in some scenarios be the first stage in transferring it into a limited company.

7.12 Taking Trading Property Stock for Your Own Use – or to Let Out

In a way, this is the reverse of the previous Case Study. If you are trading as a property developer, and you decide you would like to keep one of the houses in your trading stock (either to live in it yourself, or to let it out for the long term), you will come up against the notoriously unfair rule derived from the tax case of ***Sharkey v Wernher***, which says you are deemed to make a market value sale to yourself**.** So notoriously unfair, in fact, that it was at risk of serious challenge until it was turned into legislation – ITTOIA 2005 ss172A – F, by reason of FA 2008. I recall a very competent tax barrister offering to take cases on this point *pro bono*, and HMRC simply refused to let them be heard by a tribunal – probably because they feared they might lose. Instead, the government changed the law, arguably to spare HMRC's blushes.

If you are a property developer, therefore, and you decide to take one of your houses in stock and keep it for yourself, whether to live in or to let out, **your property development business will be taxed as if it had sold that house to you at its market value**.

The moral of this is to make your mind up quickly – ideally before you build the house - so that you can take the **land** out of the business at its (presumably much lower) market value, and then all you have to do is exclude the cost of building that house from your property development business accounts. You should ensure to keep good evidence of when the decision was made to appropriate the property from trading stock to capital / personal use. There is no option to 'postpone' the trading profit on deemed sale to yourself, until you ultimately dispose of the asset, that corresponds with the option for taking capital assets from your business, as per 7.11.

7.13 Expenses for Property Developers – "Capital v Revenue"

It is important to understand the distinction between Capital and Revenue, both for receipts and for expenses.

There have been numerous tax cases on this issue, and the distinction can be very fine in the "grey areas" between the two, but as far as the typical property letting business is concerned, the path is quite well-trodden, and there are some clear distinctions to be made.

Capital expenditure involves acquiring an "enduring asset" for your business – the most obvious example being buying a property that you intend to keep and use as the HQ of your development business.

A **Capital receipt** involves receiving a payment for disposing of such an asset – again, the most obvious example would be selling a property that you have been using as your HQ.

Revenue expenditure means expenses that do not produce an "enduring asset" – the basic running costs of your business. An obvious example would be travelling expenses.

Revenue receipts mean the income produced from the business – such as the sale of the developed properties.

You deduct **revenue expenses** from **revenue receipts** to arrive at your **profit** for **Income Tax** purposes.

You deduct **capital expenditure** from **capital receipts** to arrive at the **capital gains** you make from disposing of your "fixed assets".

As we shall see, there can sometimes be problems in deciding exactly where the line should be drawn between capital and revenue, particularly where expenditure is concerned.

Please note this section of the book for property developers applies the traditional approach to preparing accounts – the **accruals basis** – rather than the **new cash basis** for small businesses, where one focuses solely on amounts received and amounts paid out. There are two good reasons for not using the cash basis and sticking with the traditional approach: one is that the cash basis is nowhere near as straight forward as HMRC would like you to think that it is. The other is that relief for finance costs – loan interest, etc. – in the cash basis is so heavily restricted as to be almost useless to a property developer. Please see 10.4 and 10.5 for more background on these concepts.

Note also that as of 2023, HMRC is consulting on expanding the cash basis for self-employed businesses (such as property developers) so that many more traders will be brought within scope. The proposals include:

- Raising the maximum threshold at which a business can be eligible to adopt the cash basis – or even abolishing the threshold altogether
- Making it cash basis by default so that, like landlords, traders will have to elect out of the cash basis every year
- Making the current restrictions on reliefs for losses and interest costs less severe

But tellingly, HMRC's idea of reducing the severity of the interest restriction is to increase the cap from the current £500pa to, say, £1,000pa. Bearing in mind that the Base Lending Rate is now almost 10x what it was when the Cash Basis for the Self-Employed was first devised in 2013, that kind of largesse is unlikely to win many traders over (hence HMRC's proposal to apply the Cash Basis automatically, unless they elect out!)

7.14 "Wholly and Exclusively"

In order to be allowable as an expense of the development business, revenue expenditure must also have been incurred "wholly and exclusively" for the purposes of the business.

In some cases, expenses are incurred partly for the purposes of the business, and partly for other purposes.

Provided that it is possible to arrive at an objective way of apportioning the expense between business and private elements, the business part can be claimed as an expense. For example, you may use your car partly for the purpose of your business (visiting properties, etc.), and partly for private purposes. Some journeys will be wholly for business purposes, and some will be wholly private; the fraction of total motoring expenses that you choose to claim is meant to represent those **wholly business** journeys. Some journeys (and indeed other expenses) may contain a mixture of private and business purposes and may not be claimed – see 7.16 and "Duality of Purpose".

If you keep a record of your business and private mileage, you can claim the business proportion of the running costs of the car.

There are some cases where it is impossible to say that any proportion of an expense was incurred "wholly and exclusively" for the purpose of the business, even though the business was one of the reasons for the expenditure.

The classic example is clothing – it also serves the private purposes of keeping you warm and sparing your blushes. Although clothing that has a specific protective function, such as safety helmets and overalls, is an allowable expense, ordinary clothing is not.

Even if, for example, you buy cheap jeans specifically to wear on site visits, they are not allowable as an expense because they can be regarded as normal everyday clothing that serves a private purpose of keeping you warm, etc. But overalls, gloves or other items only worn when on site may well be deductible.

7.15 Allowable Expenses

Subject to the rules on capital expenditure and the "wholly and exclusively" rule, pretty much all of the expenses you incur in order to earn the profits of your property development business can be deducted to arrive at your profit.

Particular care is needed with certain types of expenditure:

- Wages and salaries for spouse or children – while it can be a tax efficient idea to employ your family in the business (because if they have little or no other income, they can use their tax-free personal allowance and lower rate bands against their wages, while those wages reduce your taxable profits), you must be able to justify the amounts you pay them as being reasonable, commercial pay for the work they do. If you clearly pay more than a commercial rate for doing work in the business, then it cannot have been incurred wholly and exclusively for business purposes. See also 7.20 Employed or Self-Employed?

- Business Entertaining of clients or prospective customers is not an allowable expense. One exception is annual staff parties or similar events – these *are* an allowable expense, as they benefit the business by promoting goodwill amongst its *employees* (and they can also be tax-free for the employees, provided the cost per head is not more than £150 for the year).

- Accountancy fees for preparing your accounts are allowable expenses. Strictly speaking, the costs of agreeing your tax liabilities are not (because they are not "wholly and exclusively" incurred to earn the profits, but rather to measure the tax once the profits have been earned).

  There is, however, a long-standing practice of allowing the costs of normal tax compliance fees.

- Training costs for your employees are generally allowable, provided there is some business benefit to the training.

  The costs of your training as the owner of the business are more problematic. If the training is merely to update you, then the cost will be allowable.

  If the training teaches the proprietor new skills, and particularly if it results in a recognised qualification, then HMRC will argue that it is a capital expense (because your new skills/qualifications are an asset of enduring benefit to the business – a capital expense) and as such not allowable.

  For example, I regularly attend training courses to keep myself up to date with the latest developments in tax, and these are an allowable expense for me.

  I am also qualified as a Chartered Tax Adviser, which involved several training courses and examinations. If I had incurred this expenditure myself as a sole trader or a partner, it would not have been allowable but, fortunately for me, it was paid for by my employers at the time. *They* will have got a deduction for the cost, because it was for training an employee – as above.

- Repairs or improvements – *repairing* the fixed assets of a business will generally be a tax-allowable business expense but *improving* an asset will not; see 10.8 Repairs and Renewals for further detail on this approach.

  Note, however, that:

  - The laptop used in the illustrative example at the beginning of 10.8 would be a typical fixed asset of a property renovation business, but
  - Repairing a *property* as per the subsequent Case Study would usually **not** be particularly problematic in terms of "Capital v Revenue", because a property developer would normally be working on a property to sell it for a trading profit – they would not be at risk of improving a capital asset of the business (unlike a property investment/rental business), because the asset they're working on is essentially trading stock.

- Travelling expenses – these deserve a section to themselves:

7.16 Travelling Expenses

If you travel "wholly and exclusively" for the purposes of your property development business, you can deduct the costs of such travel.

It is important to determine where your business is run from.

If you keep all of the paperwork at home and use your home as the office for the business, then travel from your home to any of your properties or development sites, or to another business venue (a DIY store for materials, for example) will be an allowable expense. HMRC will, however, challenge this unless you can show that your home is genuinely the place where you carry on your business. If you use a letting agent to run all your investment properties, for example, HMRC may argue that it is effectively *that agent's* office, not your home, that is your place of business.

If you have an office away from your home where you run the business, then travel from your home to that office will not be allowable, but travel from that office to other business destinations will be.

The other pitfall is "duality of purpose" – where something is **not** "wholly and exclusively" for the purposes of the business, but has some other purpose as well. If there is a substantial private benefit from your journey, HMRC will say part of its purpose was not exclusively for business, and again disallow the expenditure:

Duality of Purpose

Max lives outside Birmingham, and is engaged on a renovation in the city. He travels from home to the site, spends ten minutes discussing progress with the foreman, and then parks near the Bullring and does his weekly shopping before returning home.

Because the journey had a substantial private purpose, he cannot claim a deduction for it.

The following week, he makes the same trip to see the foreman, but this time the only other thing he does is to stop at a garage on the way, to fill up with petrol and buy a newspaper. In this case, the private benefit of the journey is clearly trivial, and so he can deduct the cost.

The cost of a journey in your car includes a proportion of the cost of running the car for the year, so you will need to keep a record of:

- Business and private mileage (perhaps keep a notebook in the car, and record the business mileage. If you also make a note of the total mileage as at 6 April and the following 5 April, you will be able to work out your business/private proportion).
- Cost of petrol, oil, screen wash, etc. **Keep the receipts.**
- Cost of insurance, MOT, Road Tax, AA/RAC membership (**Keep bank statements/documentation from the provider**)
- Cost of interest on loan used to buy car (not repayments of capital) (**loan paperwork will detail the cost of finance over the term of the loan**)

- Cost of servicing and repairs. **Keep the receipts**

You can then claim the business proportion of the above costs, together with all costs incurred directly on a business journey, such as parking and tolls.

7.17 Capital Cost of Cars and Other Capital Allowances

You can claim Capital Allowances on the cost of your car, again based on the business proportion.

The rules for expenditure on cars incurred after April 2009, are that they should be claimed at one of the two "rates" for capital allowances – the 6% rate if their CO_2 emissions are over 50g/km, or the 18% rate if their emissions are equal to or under 50g/km (as the car is first leased or acquired by your business). Note that the lower rate was 8% up until 5 April 2019. The emissions-based restriction to a lower rate applies only to cars – not to vans, etc., although certain other types of asset automatically fall within the 6% special rate pool.

Capital Allowances on Cars

Max buys a car (emissions under 50g/km CO_2) on 1 March 2023, for £16,000. For 2022/23 his Capital Allowances on the car are worked out as follows:

2022/23		**Private (90%)**	**Business (10%)**	**Deduction Allowed**
Cost of car	16,000			2022/23
WDA 18%	(2,880)	2,592	288	288
Tax cost carried forward to 2021/22	13,120			
2023/24				**2023/24**
Tax cost brought forward	13,120			
WDA 18%	(2,362)	2,126	236	236
Tax cost carried forward to 2022/23	10,758			

In 2024/25, Max sells the car for £11,000:

2024/25		**Private (90%)**	**Business (10%)**	**Balancing charge added to profits**
Tax cost brought forward	10,758			2024/25

Sale proceeds	11,000			
Balancing charge	242	218	24	24

Capital Allowances basically act to 'spread' the cost of the asset over its several-year life in the business, claiming the business proportion for each year in turn.

As the business got more back on the car on re-sale than the reduced tax cost at that point, the business has had more Capital Allowances than it should, so a balancing *charge* is made. Unlike in 2022/23 and 2023/24, where Max got a tax deduction, the charge means an addition to taxable profits in 2024/25.

If Max had got only (say) £7,000 back for the car in 2024/25, then clearly the tax allowances claimed to date would not have been enough, so he would have been entitled to another tax deduction – a balancing *allowance* – of £3,758 in that case. (£10,758 - £7,000)

Note in the above table that Max's business/private proportion remains the same each year. In practice it can vary from year to year, and the balancing charge (or balancing allowance if Max sold the car for less than its brought forward cost) would be based on the average for the period he had owned the car.

Note also that the rules for cars provided by a business to its *employees* are a little different – there is no private use adjustment, for example, because the employees are subject to a taxable car benefit for any private use (and for fuel if that is also made available for private use).

Finally, when Max comes to replace his car, he may want to consider an all-electric car (strictly, any car with 0gCO_2/km emissions) to secure special tax allowances available for **brand-new** ultra-low emissions vehicles, but they can be expensive to buy.

7.18 Alternative Method for Car Expenses Claims: Mileage

Sole traders and partners (and company directors or employees using their own car for business) are allowed to avoid all the complexity of apportioning business and private mileage, and capital allowances, by using a standard figure per **business** mile to claim their car mileage costs. For 2023/24, the rate is:

First 10,000 business miles in tax tear = 45p per mile
Subsequent business miles in tax year = 25p per mile

Note - you cannot normally switch between the strict method and the 45p/25p method from one year to the next: once you adopt one method for a particular car, you must stay with it until you change the car.

7.19 Other Capital Allowances

As a trader, you can also claim Capital Allowances on other "Plant and Machinery" you buy for the purposes of your business, such as:

- Office furniture and equipment

- Vans, lorries, etc. (these commercial vehicles do not generally suffer from the same emissions-based restrictions above as do cars, but basically all types of **brand-new** 0%-emissions vehicles are eligible for their own 100% initial allowance, up to April 2025)

- Machinery such as cement mixers, compressors, etc.

- Computers, printers, etc.

The basic principle is that you claim an "Annual Investment Allowance" of 100% ("AIA") on up to £1milllion of qualifying expenditure per year. As with basically all Capital Allowances claims, it is possible to disclaim some or all of the Allowance, so as to avoid its being wasted (such as when profits have already been reduced to the point at which they will be met by the Income Tax Personal Allowance, or perhaps create losses that cannot easily be relieved)

If you are going to spend a substantial amount on items potentially eligible for AIA, such as on vans, a lift or building equipment, even if it is "only" a few tens of thousands of pounds – always check with your adviser first!

The remaining expenditure is the subject of a "Writing Down Allowance" of (usually) 18% each year thereafter on any balance left over, following the mechanism set out in 7.17.

The AIA does **not** apply to cars, which is why Max could not claim 100% relief on the car purchase above. But if, say, he had spent £16,000 on a new pickup truck that qualified as a van, (so not a car), then he would have been able to claim all of the £16,000 in the period he bought the van. The underlying or basic 'slow' Capital Allowances mechanism set out in 7.17 applies where:

- Total expenditure on eligible plant and machinery fixed assets in the tax period exceeds the Annual Investment Allowance that is available – the traditional mechanism applies to any excess – or

- The assets in question are ineligible for the Annual Investment Allowance (typically cars), or

- The taxpayer has disclaimed some or all of the Annual Investment Allowance that is available on the expenditure on the asset(s), so the basic mechanism applies by default to the disclaimed balance (although the taxpayer can in turn disclaim some or all of the default Capital Allowances as well, so as to use the balance in a later period)

Note that certain assets with exceptionally long lives or that are "integral" to buildings will, in the absence of available AIA, only ever qualify for writing down allowances of 6%pa, as against the main rate of 18%pa. They do, however, still qualify for inclusion in the AIA of £1millionpa, so this is normally a concern only when the total expenditure is quite substantial. Where this may be the case, the taxpayer will probably allocate available AIA to those "integral feature" or long-life assets first, so that any expenditure **not** covered by that AIA falls within the more mainstream asset categories, eligible for 18%pa. See also Chapter 12 Commercial Property, for more on Capital Allowances.

There is also a new **Structures and Building Allowance (SBA)** on the capital cost of developing (or in some cases substantively extending, converting, etc.) a commercial property on or after 29 October 2018. That cost **ex**cludes land, and any expenditure which already qualifies for Capital Allowances (such as plant, machinery and other fixtures and fittings or integral features). The SBA was initially given at a flat rate of 2% per annum, so as to give relief over 50 years, but from April 2020 this was increased to a flat rate of 3% per annum. This may seem like a trivial rate, but the construction cost itself is likely to make up a very substantial part of the cost of a new commercial building, so the SBA is in turn likely to be quite valuable.

Some readers will be familiar with the old Industrial Buildings Allowance, and this new regime is effectively a much simpler version of IBAs. From a developer's perspective, while it should make brand new commercial developments significantly more attractive to buyers, nearly-new properties built prior to 29 October 2018 are likely to be much less so.

Finally, Budget 2021 announced a new "**Super Deduction**" of 130% – <u>available only to companies</u> – for qualifying expenditure on brand-new items incurred from 1 April 2021 up to 31 March 2023. This *sounds* very generous, as it effectively gave companies 19% x 130% = 24.7% tax relief. To put it another way, £100,000 invested in eligible plant would get a £19,000 reduction in Corporation Tax under the Annual Investment Allowance as above, but £24,700 under this new Super Deduction. Indeed, the Chancellor called it "bold, unprecedented action".

It could instead be argued that it actually did little more than try to persuade most companies **not** to postpone any plans to invest in qualifying plant and machinery, etc., until the new 25% CT main rate applied from 1 April 2023, by ensuring that the company basically achieved the same effective tax relief of 25% in the Super-Deduction period as it does from when the new rate started, in April 2023.

<u>For example:</u>

£100,000 of qualifying expenditure invested from 1 April 2021 up to 31 March 2023 secured tax relief of £100,000 x 130% x 19% Corporation Tax rate = £24,700.

£100,000 invested from 1 April 2023 – provided it gets 100% Annual Investment Allowance/AIA or similar – will get tax relief of £100,000 x 25% Corporation Tax Main Rate = £25,000.

Having said that, companies with annual taxable profits **below** £50,000pa are still taxable at only 19% Corporation Tax, so the Super-Deduction offers (offered) a real tax saving, for expenditure on eligible brand-new assets prior to 1 April 2023.

7.20 Employed or Self-Employed?

As part of your property development business, you may well have other people working for you.

If they are involved in "construction operations", you may already have considered the Construction Industry Scheme (CIS – see paragraph 7.7), but there is another important distinction to consider.

Caution: Note that, strictly, the first thing to consider for a new worker is **not** the CIS – this will only apply once you have satisfied yourself that the worker concerned is self-employed – working for themselves) and **not** an employee. In other words:

1) Are they now my employee? If so, then apply PAYE. If not –
2) Are we in a contractor/sub-contractor relationship? If so, then apply CIS.
3) **Only if <u>not</u> caught by either PAYE or CIS, can you pay someone "gross", without having to report payments to HMRC**

Anyone who does work for your business may be either self-employed (as you will be yourself, unless you use a company for your business), or they may be employed by you. **If they *are* an employee, then you are required to operate the PAYE system to collect tax and NIC from their wages – basically, whatever you pay them.**

Note that paying wages or salaries will usually end up costing the employer business more money as well as time, given that the employer will often have to pay Employers' NICs .

Problems often arise where a person assures you he or she is "self-employed" when in fact he should be treated by you as an employee.

Even if someone is genuinely self-employed in another capacity, he or she may be employed by you because of the terms under which he or she works for you, specifically.

The distinction between employment and self-employment can be very difficult to make. Some basic questions to ask yourself are:

- Is this person genuinely in business on his or her own account – is he able to make extra profit by doing the job efficiently, or at risk of losing money if he is inefficient? (If so, then this is indicative of self-employment).

- Does he provide his own equipment and materials? (If so, then he is more likely self-employed)

- Does he agree a price for a job, or does he charge by the hour? (A fixed price for a task is indicative of self-employment, whereas an hourly rate could apply both to self-employment or employment).

- Does he get holiday pay or sick pay? (If so, he is probably an employee).

- Does he have to do the work personally, or can he send one of his own employees or another similarly-qualified person to do it for him? (If he can genuinely "substitute" someone else for his role, he is almost certainly **not** your employee).

- Does he do a specific job for which you agree terms, or is he just available for you to use for any reasonable task? (If the latter, then he may be an employee).

- If he makes a mess of a job, or damages something, is he liable to make it good at his own time/expense? (If at his own time/expense, then this indicates he is self-employed).

- Does he do the work on his own terms (for example, you agree a deadline, but then how he meets that deadline is up to him), or does he work as and when you tell him to do so?

None of these is conclusive, except perhaps for the "substitution" test at the fifth bullet point above, but together they will build up a picture of the relationship and help to decide if it is one of employment or self-employment.

Strictly, when engaging people to work for you when they have their own companies, you will potentially have to consider the rules for "IR35" which sometimes require the engager/employer to apply PAYE when paying someone for working through their own personal services company; (e.g., if say, Ed of Edwina Current Electrical Services Limited does some electrical work for you); this started to apply to large and medium-sized private businesses from April 2021, so any 'small' business does not have to consider if IR35 applies to any of its contractors. 'Small' is actually pretty big: so long as **the hiring business** satisfies at least 2 of the following 3 criteria, it will qualify as 'small' and is not legally obliged to follow the IR35 requirements:

- Annual turnover not exceeding £10.2million
- Balance Sheet total not more than £5.1million
- Not more than 50 employees

If you have any doubts as to whether someone working for you is employed or self-employed, it is important to take advice from a tax adviser. This is because if you get it wrong, you may incur significant extra tax liabilities:

7.21 Grossing Up

Where someone wrongly treated as self-employed has received payments that should have been made under PAYE, the inspector will generally argue that the liability should be settled by the employer rather than the employee, and that this should be done by "grossing up" the payments made – reversing the normal salary calculation to deduce what the starting gross amount would have to be, to arrive at the desired net amount after tax and NI deductions.

Grossing Up

Bob has been working for you as a driver, and has been paid without deduction of PAYE, because you both wrongly thought he was self-employed. He has been paid £400 per week. It is agreed that this should have been paid under PAYE.

Bob has full tax allowances, (he has no income from other sources), so for him to have received £400 in cash, the PAYE deductions would have been:

Gross payment	473
Less Income Tax at 20%	(46)
Less Employees' NIC at 12%	(27)

Gives weekly net cash to Bob of	400

In addition, the company would have had to pay Employers' NIC at 13.8% on the £473 – another £41. So, because you paid Bob without operating PAYE, the annual amount of tax and NIC the inspector will seek to claim will be:

Weekly Income Tax	46
Weekly Employees' NIC	27
Weekly Employers' NIC	41
Weekly total	114
Times 53 gives	6,042

(Note – the PAYE year is often 53 weeks long, and also note it is HMRC practice to round down to the nearest pound). Note also that the National Insurance Costs easily exceed the Income Tax costs – **people often forget that NICs are just as expensive as the Income Tax bill, if not more so**, when it comes to grossing-up calculations.

The above amount may seem relatively manageable, but if Bob has been working for you on similar terms for the last four years, then the cost may well mount up!

"Grossing up" does not always happen – but it is almost always the position HMRC starts from, and you will need a Tax Adviser who has experience of negotiating with HMRC on these cases to ensure the damage is limited as much as possible. The other good news is that, provided Bob has paid his self-employed Income Tax and NIC, the amounts he has paid already on the income received from you can usually be set against the tax and NIC shown above.

7.22 Losses

Because property *development* is a trade, if you make a tax-adjusted loss from property development in a tax year, you can basically set this loss against any other income you may have for that year (salary, investment income, pension received, and so on), and claim repayment of any tax overpaid as a result. Usually, this can also be extended to your other income in the previous tax year, as a separate (but related) claim. In the case of losses at the beginning or end of your trading enterprise, the loss can often be carried back even further to earlier years, where profits and/or other income will hopefully have been more substantial.

The government also announced special provisions to address financial problems caused by the pandemic, so that trading loss claims arising in 2021 and 2022, could be carried back up to 3 years.

The detailed calculation of a loss for tax purposes, and how to set it off against other income – and how the loss relief may be restricted in some circumstances – can become extremely complicated: **take professional advice if you are in this situation**.

7.23 Finance Costs – Loan Interest

The basic proposition is a simple one – any interest on loans taken out "wholly and exclusively" for the purpose of financing the business is an allowable expense, as are the costs of getting those loans (re)arranged in the first place – (re)arrangement fees, valuations, guarantee fees, and so on.

This applies whatever the kind of loan involved – a mortgage, a bank loan, and even an overdraft, provided it is an overdraft on an account used solely for the business.

In order to understand the concept of "wholly and exclusively" as it applies to loan interest, however, we need to look at "the proprietor's capital account".

7.24 Proprietor's Capital Account

The proprietor's capital account is a record of the proprietor's financial relationship with his business. There is a useful accounting fiction that the business is separate from the individual who owns it. Tax rules broadly follow such fundamental accounting principles.

On the plus side, it will have any "capital introduced" into the business – such as if, when you first decide to trade as a property developer, you buy a development property for cash, using your own savings; or if, later on, you pay for business expenses out of your private resources. To this will be added the profits made each year – but if the business makes losses, these will be deducted.

On the other side, your "drawings" will be deducted – these are the sums of money you take out of the business for your own use, for private expenditure, to pay your taxes, and so on.

The basic principle is that as long as the proprietor's capital account is not overdrawn, any interest paid by the business on loans for business purposes should be an allowable expense. If it becomes overdrawn, then some of the interest <u>may</u> be disallowed. (However, please see the Caveat).

Overdrawn Capital Account

Karen sets up in business as a property developer. She buys a rundown property for £40,000, using her life savings. After spending £30,000 on renovating it (financed by a business overdraft) she sells it for £110,000, thus making a profit of £40,000. For the first year, her capital account looks like this:

Capital introduced	40,000
Add profit for year (after costs incl. overdraft)	40,000
Total	80,000
Deduct drawings:	
Income tax/NIC (say 40%)	(16,000)
Cash taken for private use	(20,000)
Balance on capital account	44,000

Note that the example assumes that the business account will fund Karen's tax bill, etc., and roughly £400 per week in personal expenses. Clearly, Karen had other income sources in that first year, if she was already paying tax at (roughly) 40%.

Karen's capital account with this business is not overdrawn, so all of the overdraft interest paid on the business overdraft is an allowable expense.

Even if Karen had decided to treat herself to some expensive luxuries, she could have spent up to another £44,000 (financed from the business overdraft if she wanted) and all the interest would still be allowable.

Karen continues trading for some years, financing the business via the overdraft

She then has a couple of bad years where she makes losses, but as the business is now her only source of income, she still has to draw cash for her living expenses.

In year 3, her capital account looks like this:

Balance from previous year	30,000
Deduct loss for year	(20,000)
Total	10,000
Deduct drawings:	
Income tax/NIC (nil – losses)	NIL
Cash for private use	(20,000)
Capital account overdrawn	(10,000)

Because Karen's capital account is now overdrawn, HMRC may argue that part of the overdraft interest is being used to finance her private lifestyle, as represented here by her drawings of £20,000, and the interest should therefore **not be** allowable as a deduction against profits – in this example, reducing the loss she has made, for tax purposes.

This is a simplified calculation: the exact amount of the interest that will be disallowed is quite complex and adjustments are required for things like losses and depreciation, but the principle should be clear – if your accumulated drawings are greater than the money you put into the business at the start plus the profits you have made to date, then HMRC will argue that some of the loans are financing your drawings – private expenditure – and not the business.

Caveat: It should be noted that, at the time of writing, HMRC seems to want to re-interpret its own long-standing guidance, now to require in particular that **any additional sums borrowed are used specifically and demonstrably within that business**, for business purposes, otherwise interest relief will not be allowed, even if the capital account is *not* overdrawn. This certainly seems to be HMRC's position for one unfortunate BTL investor whose claim for tax relief has been resisted by HMRC, according to some relatively recent articles in the tax press. As this is a "developing issue", you should speak to your adviser to make sure you have the most up to date guidance, if you think this may affect your tax position.

Having recently taken a similar case as far as HMRCs "Alternative Dispute Resolution" process, the author's own experience suggests that this is down to individual officers' reliance on poorly-composed updates to that formerly-reliable guidance, and **this re-interpretation should be strongly resisted**.

Note: The rules for interest, etc., in companies "Loan Relationships" – are quite different in the mechanics, but the fundamental principle that the cost of loans taken out for business purposes should be allowable, is essentially the same.

7.25 Loans for Mixed Purposes and Using "Mixed Accounts"

Where possible, it is best to avoid using loans on accounts that are mainly used for private purposes, as this can lead to complications.

For example, if you use your private credit card to pay for business expenses, you can treat those expenses as part of the "capital introduced" into the business, as described above. If you want to claim a deduction for the interest on the credit card, however, you would need to treat the whole of the credit card account as part of your capital account with the business, in order to differentiate the business elements, and private elements (which would basically go to drawings).

This is possible in theory, but potentially very difficult in terms of the accounting entries required to manage potentially a large number of individual transactions. It is therefore much better to have a credit card that you use solely for business expenses, and include this in the business accounts – then all the interest will be allowable, subject to the rule about not overdrawing your capital account described above.

Having said that, if you were to extend your mortgage on your home to finance your business, for example, then it would almost certainly be worth claiming for the corresponding business proportion of your mortgage interest, despite the complications!

7.26 Partnerships

Instead of being a sole trader, you may set up your property development business as a partnership – trading together with one or more other people, and sharing the risks and rewards with them. If you decide to do this, there are some important tips to bear in mind:

- Have a written partnership agreement – if you do not, then the Partnership Act 1890 will govern how profits and losses are split and, depending on the circumstances, it can presume that they will be split equally between the partners – which may not be what you want.
- Beware of taking children into partnership unless they genuinely contribute to the business
- Provided the documents are correctly drafted, however, it is very difficult for HMRC to challenge a spouse as partner.
- Take advice from a tax adviser on the finer points of how to deal with the partnership's tax – it can be a complicated area, with traps for the unwary!
- Always take advice before making any changes to the partnership – such as who is a partner, what the profit shares are, and so on – again, beware there are numerous pitfalls!

Caution: Keep in mind that general partners are "**jointly liable**" for the debts of a normal partnership – **if one partner cannot pay, a creditor can go after the other partner(s) for the full amount due, including claiming against that other partner's private assets**.

You need to be able to trust anyone you go into partnership with! (And have a partnership agreement).

Alternatively, take advice on setting up a "Limited Liability Partnership" or "LLP" – as the name suggests, it restricts the individual partner's personal liability.

8 Taxation for Homeowners

For many people, their home is their most valuable asset, and all the more valuable because they believe that when they sell it, they will make a capital gain that is exempt from tax.

In this part of the guide, we will look at the details of how that tax exemption works, and what pitfalls and opportunities it provides. We will also look at an exemption from income tax on rental income from your home ("Rent-a-Room Relief" – see 8.9).

We will start with the basic rules, and then look at what can be done with them:

8.1 The Basic Exemption

It is common knowledge that you are exempt from Capital Gains Tax (CGT) on a gain you make from selling your home.

As we shall see, this exemption is quite a bit more complicated than it might appear.

8.2 "Only or Main Residence"

The exemption (strictly, it is a relief) applies to a person's "only or main residence" (also referred to as one's "Principal Private Residence", or "PPR").

In a simple case where a person owns only one property, lives in it as his or her home, and does not use it for any other purpose then, when he sells it, he will pay no CGT.

A person can basically have only one main residence at a time, and a married couple (or civil partnership) can have only one such PPR between them.

If a person (or couple) has more than one property that could be regarded as a main residence, they have the opportunity to "nominate" which one the tax relief should apply to. As we shall see, it is <u>vital</u> to make this nomination within the time limit that applies. See also 9.2 on what makes a property a main residence.

Since April 2015, you can be charged to CGT on the disposal of residential property you own even though you are not resident in the UK – "Non-Resident CGT", or "NRCGT". You can still avoid the charge, if that residential property qualifies as your main residence during your period of ownership, however **if you are not UK-resident then you can basically nominate a property in the UK as a main residence only if you spend at least 90 nights there in the tax year in question**. Similar rules apply if you are resident in the UK but wish to nominate a non-UK property as your main residence. You should seek tailored advice when you intend to claim on a non-UK property, or to claim on a UK property as a non-resident individual, as the rules and calculations can become complex.

The NRCGT regime has effectively been extended to cover disposals of commercial property from April 2019, along similar lines – but that will not normally be relevant to homeowners, nor to property developers, since developing property other than one's main home would generally be part of his or her trading activity, and therefore subject to Income Tax rather than to CGT. See also 5.2 for a brief summary of the regime for non-residents disposing of UK land, in relation to notifying HMRC and paying CGT on account.

Companies cannot have an "only or main residence". In some cases, a Trust may hold a property on behalf of a beneficiary/ies who want to occupy it as their main residence, but there are restrictions on the relief, and you should take professional advice to ensure that the Trust and PPR relief will apply as expected.

8.3 "Garden or Grounds"

The exemption covers not only the house itself, but also the "permitted area" of the land around it. This may lead to the quite attractive prospect of selling a development plot out of a large garden or similar, free of CGT, while retaining one's main residence (see also 9.1).

Up to half a hectare (about 1.2 acres) of garden-plus-grounds is allowed by statute, but a larger area **may** be included in the exemption if it is "required for the reasonable enjoyment" of the property "having regard to the size and character of the dwelling-house".

The issue of what area of land larger than half a hectare is required for the "reasonable enjoyment" of your home has led to numerous tax cases being tried in the Courts, and it would be pointless to go into the details here as each case is different, (although Phillips v HMRC [2020] UKFTT 0381 (TC) may well prove informative) but there is one particular point that is worth keeping in mind:

Sale of Part Grounds

Mr Grey and Mr Green live in similar large houses. Each house has a garden of 1.7 acres.

Mr Grey sells his house (and garden). There is some discussion with the inspector about whether the "extra" half acre (above the 1.2-acre limit) is "required for the reasonable enjoyment" of the property, but the inspector eventually concedes that it is, and the whole gain is exempt.

Mr Green receives an excellent offer to sell a half-acre of his garden to a property developer.

He has read about CGT, so he knows that because he still owns the house, the exemption for the garden or grounds can apply to this sale.

He sells the land, and does not expect to pay CGT on the gain he makes.

The tax inspector does not agree, and says that CGT is due on the substantial gain Mr Green made on selling the half acre.

Mr Green objects that when his friend Mr Grey sold a similar house and land, it was accepted that the whole gain was exempt.

"Ah", replies the tax inspector, "but the test must be applied to the exact circumstances of each sale, and to me, the very fact that you are prepared to sell that half acre while you remain living in the house <u>may be prima facie evidence that the part disposed of was **not *required*** for the reasonable enjoyment of the dwelling house as a residence.</u> So the exemption doesn't apply to it".

(The underlined words above are taken directly from HMRC's own CGT Manual at paragraph CG64832).

See also 9.1 below.

8.4 Periods of Absence

Generally speaking, a property is only your main residence while you are actually living there, but there are certain exceptions:

- You can be absent for up to three years (either continuously or for several shorter periods up to a total of three years) for any reason, and
- You can be absent for any period during which you (or your spouse or civil partner) are employed in a full-time job outside the UK, and
- You can be absent for up to four years if your (spouse's, civil partner's, etc.) place of work makes this necessary (whether you are employed or self-employed)

For any of these three exceptions to apply, there are two conditions which must normally be fulfilled:

- The property must have been your main residence at some time both before and after the period of absence (there are exceptions in some cases)
- You must not have had another main residence during the period of absence (this is one example of how important the "nomination" of your main residence can be).

Absences from Main Residence

James Bond buys a house in London in March 2002, and lives in it as his main residence until January 2003. He then leaves the house and is away until he returns to it in December 2005 (he prefers not to say where he was, but during 2003 the inspector of taxes received a letter from him from the Cayman Islands, saying that he had a lease on a flat there and he wished to "nominate" his London property as his main residence).

From January 2006 until December 2011, he is away in Russia, working for the British Embassy in Moscow. He lives in various different hotels – a hotel room cannot normally be a "main residence"

Mr Bond returns to the UK in December 2011, and in January 2012 he sets up a business in the Scottish Highlands, offering "adventure training" and "team building" for business executives. He rents a castle to accommodate this business. He also makes another main residence nomination in favour of his London house.

In December 2015, Mr Bond returns to the London house, and moves back in. He lives there until March 2023, when he sells the property.

All of the gain is exempt, because:

- His "unexplained" absence lasted just under three years
- While he was away in Moscow, he had a full-time job there (note there is no time limit for this type of absence)
- He obviously had to live in Scotland while he was running his adventure training centre, and that period lasted just under four years

And the house was his main residence both before and after all of these periods of absence, and he did not have another main residence during any of his absences – or if he did, he had "nominated" the London house. Note: if Mr. Bond's Cayman Islands 'stint' had been after April 2015, then it is still possible to use the periods of absence rules to his benefit, despite the new NRCGT regime (see 8.2) but the rules become more complex, and one would hope that he could find time in his busy schedule both to tarry awhile at his London home and for a conversation or two with a competent tax adviser...

8.5 "Job-Related Accommodation"

There is a slightly different (and more generous) relief that applies if you live in "job-related accommodation."

This relief is not often available, because the definition of "job-related accommodation" is very strict, so we will not go into great detail here.

The object of the relief is to enable someone who has to live in a particular place – such as the manager of a pub required to live on the premises – to buy a house elsewhere (perhaps for his or her retirement) and have it treated as if it is their main residence even though he or she has not yet lived there. The regime has been extended also to cover serving members of the Armed Forces who are required to live (and rent accommodation) away from home.

In some circumstances, this relief is also available to the self-employed and (in very limited circumstances) to owner/directors of companies.

Provided that it was genuinely your intention to live in the house in the future, it is possible for the house to be sold and the gain to be exempt, even if you have never in fact lived there – but HMRC are likely to look very closely at the facts in such a case.

Caution: A word of caution – if you think you may be in this situation, do not just assume your accommodation is "job-related" and that you will qualify for this relief – check with a tax adviser, as the rules are strict, complicated, and illogical, like a lot of tax rules. And make sure to keep records as evidence of your intention.

8.6 "The 9 Month Rule"

If a property has been your main residence at any time while you owned it, it is deemed to be your main residence for the last 9 months of your ownership, whether you live there during that period or not: We shall see how this rule can be made to work for you in a moment. (Note that, for disposals prior to 6 April 2020, it was the last 18 months, and for disposals prior to April 2014, it was 36 months!)

8.7 Nominating Your Main Residence

If you have more than one property that could be regarded as your main residence, you can "nominate" which property is to get the tax relief by writing to HMRC within two years of the time when the situation first arises.

For example, many people have a family home in one place, and work during the week in another place, where they have a flat. Either of these could be regarded as their residence, so they can nominate which one will get the tax relief.

The two-year time limit is strictly enforced by HMRC, so do not delay in making your nomination. If you miss the deadline, you cannot make a nomination until your situation changes – such as when you acquire another property that could be your main residence.

Note that a rented flat *could* in some cases be regarded as your main residence, so if you rent a flat during the week and return to your home at weekends, you need to nominate the home you own as your main residence. If you are in this situation and have missed the two-year deadline, one theoretical solution would be to move to another rented flat – that would start a new two-year period for a nomination. There is also a concessionary treatment that may potentially apply – and may be cheaper than renting another flat.

If you do not nominate which property is your main residence, the issue has to be decided "on the facts of the case". In other words, you may be in for a long and expensive argument with HMRC if they disagree with you as to how to interpret those facts!

Once your nomination is in place, you can "vary" it **at any time** by writing to HMRC again, and the variation can be retrospective for up to two years.

The facility to "nominate" a main residence, and then vary that nomination, can produce some substantial tax savings:

Nominating Your Main Residence

9 Month Final Period (as took effect for disposals from April 2020)

Joanne owns a large house in Devon, where she lives with her family. She and her wife bought this house in March 2011. In January 2025, she gets a job in London, and in March 2026, she buys a small flat in London (in joint names) for £200,000, where she lives during the working week, returning to Devon most weekends, while the family comes to London at other times.

Joanne writes to HMRC in March 2026, nominating the Devon house as the main residence with immediate effect. Her wife has to sign the nomination as well (it affects her too, because a married couple can only have one main residence).

In January 202**8**, Jo starts thinking about returning to Devon and starts to look for another job there. Realising that she may well end up selling the London flat for a decent gain, she writes to HMRC, saying she wants to vary the nomination, making the London flat their main residence from March 202**7**. (Once a valid nomination has been made, it can be varied, to take effect from a date up to 2 years prior to the variation).

In December 2028, she finds another job back in Devon, so she writes again, saying she wishes to vary the nomination yet again, to make the Devon house their main residence from March 2028. Her wife signs both these nominations as well, remember. They sell the London flat for £270,000 in March 2029, making a gain of £70,000.

Because of the way they have varied the nomination, the flat was occupied as their nominated main residence for tax purposes for 12 months (March 2027 to February 2028 inclusive).

But this in turn means that **the last 9 months of their ownership of it are also exempt from CGT** under the "last 9 months" rule (8.6), being July 2028 to March 2029. As they have only owned the flat for three years, 21 out of 36 months' ownership are exempt from CGT – about 60%. The gain will be around £29,000 and, assuming that they couple are able to use both CGT Annual Exemptions (currently £6,000), the CGT bill will come to around £5,000 (depending on the rate(s) applicable to their respective gains). **Note, however, that since there *is* CGT to pay on the flat, they will have to notify HMRC under the new 60-day regime as set out in 5.2, when they come to sell it.**

When Joanne and her wife eventually come to sell the Devon house, it will have been their main residence for the whole period of ownership, except for that 12-month period to March 2028, so only a small fraction of the gain will *not* be exempt from CGT, and may well be covered by their respective CGT Annual Exemptions.

If, say, they sell the Devon house in March 2031, they will have owned it for 20 years, which is 240 months, so only 12/240th of the gain will **not** be exempt – even if they made a gain of £450,000, only 22,500 of that would be taxable, and their annual exempt amounts will cover a good proportion of that (Jo and her wife are **each** entitled to £6,000 tax free capital gains in 2023/24, totalling £12,000 – although it is currently scheduled to fall to as little as £3,000 each from April 2024).

This Case Study shows that, so long as you intend to remain in your 'original' residence for long enough, it is possible to use nominations and the deemed final period of occupation on a more short-term residence that you own, so as to minimise exposure to the short-term gain, without storing up too great a problem for the future disposal of the original residence. Furthermore, if you never intend to leave the original property – if it is the home you intend to retire to – then bearing in mind that there is currently no CGT on death, you may be able to afford to be much more flexible in your nominations for short-term property ownership.

Of course, it is essential that you seek proper advice to ensure that you minimise the risk of making taxable gains in the future, depending on which

property is making gains (increasing in value) the faster/est, and for how long you intend to live in the property/ies.

For example, readers may have noticed that, had Joanne and her family been confident that the Devon property would be their "forever home", they *could* have backdated the first nomination of the London property to start from much earlier, say in 2026, and further reduced their CGT exposure when the flat was sold in 2029, with potentially little CGT risk to their first home. But these calculations are very much dependent on the specific facts of each case, as known at the time.

8.8 CGT Relief for Letting – Warning

If a property has been your main residence, and at some other stage in your ownership it has been let as "residential accommodation" while it was *not* your main residence, then a further relief from CGT is ostensibly available on the part of the gain that is attributable to the period of letting. While it remains potentially useful in some cases, its utility has been severely restricted by Finance Act 2020.

The relief is the smallest of:

- The gain due to the letting
- The amount of the gain that is exempt as your main residence
- £40,000

Finance Bill 2020 curtailed the availability of letting relief so that, for any disposals **from April 2020, it will apply only when the owner remains in occupation of the residence alongside the tenant**. The change is retrospective, meaning that the new co-occupation criterion will also be applied to any period of letting that arose even before the new conditions were introduced.

The implication is that many periods during which a person's main residence was let *before* 6 April 2020 – and would have qualified at the time – will no longer qualify for lettings relief as and when the property is disposed of on or after 6 April 2020, and lettings relief is actually claimed. When it was put to the government that this retroactive measure was unfair and lettings relief under the original regime should be preserved for periods prior 6 April 2020, it said "to do so would have added significant complexity for both taxpayers and HMRC". I suspect it is a complexity that most homeowners who could have used that relief, would have been happy to struggle through.

The first Case Study shows how lettings relief applied for disposals prior to April 2020. If sold now, even though Chris would have qualified for lettings relief at the time he let his property, that period would be ineligible.

Relief for Letting **Old Rules**

Chris bought a house in January 2012, and lived in it as his main residence until December 2013.

He then let the entire property, while living elsewhere, from January 2014 until December 2019, when he sold the house, making a gain of £160,000.

He has owned the house for 8 years.

For 3 ½ years, it was his main residence (2011 and 2012, when he actually lived there, and July 2017 to December 2018, under the "last 18 months" rule – it was sold before the "last 18 months rule" became the "last 9 months rule", as per 8.6 above, effective April 2020).

7/16 of the gain (£70,000) is therefore exempt, leaving a chargeable gain of £90,000.

The amount of the lettings exemption is therefore the smallest of:

- The gain due to the letting = £90,000
- The amount of the exemption for main residence given = £70,000
- The maximum amount of the exemption = £40,000

Chris gets the maximum exemption of £40,000, leaving only £50,000 taxable.

If Chris were married and his wife owned the house 50:50 with him, the gain would be split between them, and each of them would be entitled to their own letting relief of up to £40,000:

	Chris	**Wife**	**Total**
Gain	80,000	80,000	160,000
7/16 exempt as main residence	(35,000)	(35,000)	(70,000)
Taxable	45,000	45,000	90,000
Lettings relief = lowest of • Taxable = 45,000 • OMR exemption = 35,000 • Maximum relief = 40,000	(35,000)	(35,000)	(70,000)
Chargeable gain (covered by £12,000 annual exemption as applied in 2019/20)	10,000	10,000	20,000

Thanks to Finance Act 2020, the relief will be available – including for letting periods prior to April 2020 – only when the owner has remained in occupation of the property while the property was being let.

Lettings Relief for Co-Occupation (post-April 2020)

John buys a large house, with five bedrooms.

After a year during which he used the whole house as his main residence and used the extra bedrooms when he had parties, he offers two of his spare bedrooms out as accommodation together with kitchenette and en suite facilities, but continues to occupy the rest of the house as his main residence. He sells the house many years later and makes a gain of £250,000.

It is agreed with HMRC that the let rooms represented 20% of the value of the house, so 80% of the gain (£200,000) is exempt and 20% (£50,000) is taxable.

The letting relief is the smallest of:

- Taxable due to letting = £50,000
- Exempt as main residence = £200,000
- Maximum relief = £40,000

So £40,000 relief is given, leaving John with a taxable gain of £10,000 (subject to his Annual Exemption)

NOTE: the updated version of lettings relief will not be available where the letting is exclusively used as part of a business, so will not normally apply to more formal arrangements, including B&Bs or similar scenarios. **Contemporaneous expert advice is essential, not least because HMRC's published understanding of how the new regime will work seems at odds with what the legislation actually says!**

8.9 Income Tax Relief for Letting – "Rent a Room Relief"

Normally, if you let part of your house, you will be liable to Income Tax on the rental income (less expenses – more on this later), but there is a relief called "Rent a Room" relief which can apply to exempt up to **£7,500** of rent, per year, from tax. (It was increased in the Summer 2015 Budget, from £4,250, with effect from 6 April 2016)

The relief applies if your tenant lives with you (as with a lodger), or if they have a self-contained part of the house, <u>provided the separation of their part is only temporary, and does not involve structural alterations.</u>

The relief is not compulsory – you can elect not to have it if you wish:

Rent a Room Relief

Anne, Barry, and Chris are next door neighbours, each living in a terraced house. During the tax year 2023/24 (the year ending 5 April 2024), they each have a lodger.

Anne's lodger pays her £120 per week. Her expenses (including an appropriate proportion of the mortgage interest on the house) are £1,200 for the year

Barry's lodger pays £175 per week, to include meals. Barry has no mortgage, and his annual expenses are £1,000

Chris' lodger pays him the same as Barry's, but because he has a very large mortgage, and provides more expensive food, etc., for the lodger, his expenses are £8,400 for the year.

Anne's profit from the rental is £5,040 (£6,240 less £1,200). She is exempt from tax on this, as the gross rental income of £6,000 (not just the profit) was less than the Rent a Room limit of £7,500.

There is no point in her electing for the relief not to apply, as then she would be taxed on £5,040. Only in the unlikely event that you make a loss is it worth opting out of the scheme if your rents are less than the limit.

Barry's gross rental income of £9,100 is above the £7,500 limit. He has a choice:

- He can pay tax on his actual profit of £8,100 (£9,100 less £1,000 actual expenses) or
- He can elect to be taxed on the excess of his **gross** rental income received over the Rent a Room limit - £9,100 less £7,500 = £1,600. Clearly, this is the better option for him

Like Barry, Chris' income is above the limit, so he has a similar choice:

- Tax on actual profit of £700 (52 x £175 = £9,100 less £8,400 = £700
- Tax on rents less £7,500 = £9,100 - £7,500 = £1,600

Chris will **not** elect for the relief to apply, as he is better off paying tax as if Rent-a-Room did not exist.

NOTE 1: Whether or not you need to make an election depends on whether your rental income (not your profit) is above or below the limit for the year of £7,500.

- If it is below £7,500, you will be in the scheme unless you elect for it not to apply to you (perhaps because you have made a loss)
- If it is above £7,500, you will not be in the scheme and will be taxed in the normal way (income less allowable expenses) unless you elect to be in (probably because your actual expenses were less than £7,500, like Barry's)

NOTE 2: The £7,500 limit applies to one person's income from letting part of his main residence.

If the residence is shared and another person also gets rental income from the same residence, the amount of relief for each individual is reduced to £3,750 – so if Anne, Barry, and Chris shared one big house, and they had a lodger, their rent a room relief would be £3,750 each (it does not get further restricted below £3,750 if there are three or more landlords involved).

NOTE 3: Some readers may recall that the government tried to float a "shared occupation" requirement for Rent-a-Room Relief in July 2018 but withdrew it in October 2018, after the tax profession had denounced the proposal as unworkable. Which, given the new shared occupancy requirement that now applies for lettings relief for CGT from 6 April 2020, (see 8.8), just goes to show that you cannot teach an old dog new tricks.

8.10 Restrictions on Main Residence Relief

We have already seen that relief from CGT for your main residence can be restricted if you let part of it, or if there is a period of absence when it is not your main residence (although there are potential adjustments to be made in either of these scenarios)

A similar restriction applies where you use part of the property exclusively for the purposes of a business – a good example is a pub where the owner lives on the premises.

The apportionment is to be done on a "just and reasonable" basis:

Apportionment

The "Tax Inspector's Head" is a popular pub, owned and run by Mr Porter.

It consists of a ground floor with two bars, a ladies' and a gents' lavatory, a storeroom-cum-beer-cellar and a kitchen that is used both to prepare pub food and to cook meals for the Porter family. There are six rooms upstairs, used as their main residence by the Porter family, except for one small room which is Mr Porter's office.

When working out how to apportion the gain when the pub is sold, the following points will be relevant:

- The floor areas of the various rooms; values of the respective areas
- The fact that it is probably true that a significant part of the sale price was for the goodwill of the pub business (so not eligible for main residence relief)
- The kitchen should be treated as part of the main residence, not the business (because it was not used "exclusively" for the business as the Porters' own meals were cooked there)

- Mr Porter may argue that his office was not "exclusively" used as such and should also be excluded from the business – this will depend on the facts of the case.

8.11 Possible Refusal of Main Residence Relief

There is a potentially dangerous piece of legislation (Section 224 (3) of the Taxation of Chargeable Gains Act 1992), which says that the relief from CGT for a main residence:

"...shall not apply in relation to a gain if the acquisition of, or of the interest in, the dwelling house or the part of a dwelling house was made wholly or partly for the purpose of realising a gain from the disposal of it, and shall not apply in relation to a gain so far as attributable to any expenditure which was incurred after the beginning of the period of ownership and was incurred wholly or partly for the purpose of realising a gain from the disposal"

Just take a moment and read that through again, and then we shall have a look at what it means in practice.

Essentially, it seems to say that you don't get the CGT exemption at all, if one of your reasons ("wholly or partly") for buying the house was that you hoped you would make a profit when you eventually sold it; also, that if you spend money on improvements (new conservatory, swimming pool, etc.) and one of your reasons for that is to increase the value of the house, then you lose the exemption on that increase in value.

Fortunately, HMRC do not apply this legislation as strictly as that – their own instruction manual tells inspectors not to be "unreasonable and restrictive" in the way they apply this rule.

Merely because you buy a house hoping it will increase in value, or because you improve it partly because this will improve the selling price, you will **not** fall foul of this rule.

Examples where you *will,* are:

- Pseudo property dealing
- "Enfranchisement" of a leasehold property shortly before sale
- Property development involving your home

We will look at these in turn:

8.12 Pseudo Property Dealing

If you buy a property intending to sell it in the short term at a profit, this is normally a trading activity, but if you buy the property and live in it as your main residence, it is very difficult for HMRC to argue that you bought it as trading stock.

For example, a builder might buy a property to live in, spend a few months or more improving it, sell it on for a substantial gain and claim that it was his or her only or main residence and that the gain should not be taxed.

HMRC may struggle to say that he is trading, because it may genuinely be his main residence for that period of a few months, or a year, etc., but they will then use section 224 (3) to deny him the main residence exemption for the capital gains he makes on each house. (If this happens on several occasions, so as arguably to create a pattern, then HMRC is likely to try to contend that at least some of the transactions are trading and subject to Income Tax and NICs, taking them outside the scope of CGT entirely – and thereby denying main residence relief).

We shall shortly be looking at exactly what makes a property your main residence, and the thorny question of how long you have to live there to get the relief, but at this point, note that even if you do live at the house so that it is your main residence, if you only own the property for a short time, you may be vulnerable to losing the exemption on the basis that you bought the property with a view to making a gain on selling it.

8.13 Enfranchisement of Leasehold Property

If you are a leasehold tenant, you may get the opportunity to buy the freehold from your landlord and thus "enfranchise" your property. Especially if your lease does not have many years to run, this can considerably increase the value of your property.

If you then sell the property within the next couple of years or so, HMRC may well argue that the cost of buying the freehold was "incurred wholly or partly for the purpose of realising a gain from the disposal".

You will of course argue that you had no thought of selling at the time, and you just wanted security, and the opportunity to leave the house to your children, but the shorter the period between enfranchisement and sale, the harder this argument will be to justify.

If it is agreed that you did ("partly") think in terms of a bigger profit when you sold, the restriction on your relief will be calculated like this:

Enfranchisement

Fred lives in a leasehold property which is his main residence. The lease, which now has 65 years left to run, cost him £70,000 ten years ago. He gets the opportunity to buy the freehold for £80,000, does so, and sells the house freehold for £200,000.

After negotiations with HMRC, it is agreed that if he had not enfranchised his property, and had merely sold the 65-year lease, he would only have got £75,000 for the property.

The calculation is therefore:

Sale proceeds of freehold	200,000
Sale proceeds if leasehold only	(75,000)
Gain attributable to enfranchisement	125,000

Cost of buying freehold	(80,000)
Gain not exempt from CGT	45,000

The rest of the gain is exempt as his main residence.

NOTE: This Case Study provides the opportunity to make an important point about tax planning, often referred to as "letting the tax tail wag the dog".

Fred will pay CGT on this £45,000 gain of about £11,000, so he has a little under £110,000 in the bank, after taking account of the cost of the freehold and the CGT. If he had simply sold his lease, he would have had just £75,000, despite having paid no tax.

JUST BECAUSE YOU WILL PAY MORE TAX IF YOU UNDERTAKE A TRANSACTION, THAT DOESN'T MEAN YOU SHOULD NOT DO IT – If you will still be better off after the extra tax, then tax is no reason not to go ahead!

Note, however, that Fred will have to notify and pay HMRC on account of his CGT bill, within 60 days of completion of sale, since October 2021 (see 5.2 above)

9 Property Development of Your Home

This is the third of the three scenarios set out above, where restriction on PPR relief may apply. The commonest example is where the owner of a large home divides it up into flats before selling:

Home Divided into Flats

Barney owns a large three storey house, which he lives in as his main residence. It cost him £100,000 twenty years ago. The property is currently worth £300,000.

He decides to sell, and his estate agent suggests that if he splits the property up into three self-contained flats, he will realise a better price than he would get if he sold the house as it is.

Barney spends £50,000 on dividing the house into three flats, and then sells them for £150,000 each. If he had just sold the house as it was, he would have got £300,000 for it. Clearly, he has undertaken this development just before sale, to get a better price for his former main residence, so it is not covered by PPR relief.

The non-exempt part of the gain is calculated like this:

Sale proceeds of three flats	450,000
Sale proceeds if house sold unconverted	(300,000)
Gain attributable to conversion	150,000
Less cost of conversion	(50,000)
Gain not exempt	100,000

The gain that Barney would have made if he had just sold his property unconverted remains tax-free. Barney might also want to read Chapter 7 above, to secure reduced rates of VAT for construction costs when changing the number of dwellings (see 7.9). He would also have just 60 days to notify HMRC and account for the CGT payable, as per 5.2.

Note Barney is protected from the "transactions in land" regime because he is developing land/property that qualifies as his main residence – specifically excepted under the 'new' ITTOIA 2005 s 517M (see Chapter 6).

There is no equivalent to this exception in the corresponding Corporation Tax Act sections for companies – but putting the development into a corporate wrapper would almost certainly put the project onto a trading footing anyway, as that would be the company's "raison d'etre" (Entrepreneurs' Relief – aka Business Asset Disposal Relief – might also then be available, however.)

9.1 Selling the Garden

Sometimes it is possible to sell part of your garden, perhaps to a property developer. If the total area of your garden before this sale is less than half a hectare (about 1.2 acres – see "Garden or Grounds" at 8.3 above) then, assuming the house qualifies as your main residence, a gain on the sale of part of the garden will be exempt from CGT.

This only works if the house is your main residence at the time you sell the piece of garden.

Sale of Part of Garden

Mary's main residence has a garden of one acre. She is planning to sell the house, and she receives an offer from a developer to buy a half-acre of the garden.

While she is still negotiating with the developer, she receives an offer for the house and the remaining half acre of garden, which she accepts.

Mary exchanges contracts to sell the house on 1 March 2023, and the house is conveyed to its new owner on 21 March 2023. This gain will be exempt from CGT, because the house was Mary's main residence.

She finally agrees terms with the developer on 1 April 2023, and sells him the half acre. The capital gain on this sale is NOT exempt from CGT, because at the time of the sale, the land was NOT part of the garden of her main residence (because she had already sold the house).

If only Mary had sold the garden to the developer first, and *then* sold the house, both gains would likely have been exempt from CGT.

NOTE: The date of a sale for CGT purposes is generally the date contracts are exchanged rather than the date the sale is completed (although for the purposes of PPR Relief, FA 2020 updated the rules for a person's "period of ownership", following Higgins v HMRC [2019] EWCA Civ 1869).

But while the date of sale is usually fixed at the point of exchange, it may also be said that the sale does not actually happen unless and until the sale is "completed". Therefore the date of completion is also important.

If, in the above example, Mary had sold the garden on 10 March (after she had exchanged contracts to sell the house, but before she moved out of it when completion of the sale took place on 21 March) HMRC might have accepted that the garden was still part of her main residence on 10 March and the gain could have been exempt. Every now and again, dates *really* matter.

9.2 What is a "Main Residence"?

Throughout the last few sections we have been talking about a person's "main residence", but what exactly does this term mean?

Your main residence may be a house, or a flat.

You may own the freehold, have a lease, or merely be renting it, perhaps as a Shorthold Tenant.

Note: even rented property can be a main residence for tax purposes, and so (subject to certain restrictions – see 8.2 above) can a property outside the UK.

In order to be your main residence, a property must be occupied by you as your home, but it need not be so occupied every day – see also 8.4.

A question often asked is: how long does one have to live in a property before it becomes one's main residence, but unfortunately it is impossible to answer that question, although in the right circumstances the period of occupation can be as little as a few months, or even less.

What is important is not so much the length of time, but more the quality of the occupation of the property.

A Main Residence for a week?

Jack exchanges contracts to buy a small flat on 1 August, and the sale completes and he moves in on 21 August. He fully intends to make the flat his permanent home, but on 28 August he wins £1,000,000 on the lottery.

Jack lets the flat while he goes on a world cruise for three months, and on his return he buys a large house to live in, and sells the flat.

HMRC might be a little suspicious, but provided they could be convinced that Jack really intended to live in the flat when he bought it, and that he did actually live there for a period before his circumstances changed when he won the lottery, then any gain Jack makes on the sale of the flat should be exempt from CGT.

The key point is that, when Jack rolled up on 21 August, he occupied the property as his home and his demonstrable intention at the time was to live there, for the foreseeable future.

Useful cases 'proving' this point are Morgan v HMRC [2013] UKFTT 181 (TC) and more recently Davidson v HMRC [2019] UKFTT 300 (TC).

People who own a rental property they have never lived in are often advised to move into it before selling it, in order to get the "last 9 months" exemption and/or potentially the £40,000 "lettings exemption" (but with due regard to the **caveat** above about recent changes to the legislation, effective April 2020 – see "The 9 Month Rule" at 8.6 and "Relief for Letting" at 8.8 above):

The Last 9 Months Exemption

Mark and Mandy own a house which they have never previously lived in, but have let out. They also own their main residence. The let house cost £100,000 in May 2018. In November 2021, Mark and Mandy let out their main residence, and move into the house they had previously been letting. They live there for a year, before moving in November 2022 to a third property to follow Mandy's employment, and then sell the house in May 2023 for £300,000. The gain is calculated like this:

Sale proceeds	300,000
Less cost	(100,000)
Gain	200,000
Main residence exemption: 12 months' actual occupation to October 2022 + final 6 months (November 2022 – May 2023) deemed to have occupied (see 8.6) = 1.5 out of 5 years	(60,000)
Chargeable gain	140,000
Annual exempt amounts (couple)	(12,000)
Gain charged to tax	128,000
CGT at 28%	35,840

If Mark and Mandy had not lived in the house before they sold it, their initial gain of £200,000 would in effect have been fully taxable – after their annual exempt amounts were deducted, they would pay CGT of £52,640. Again, Mark and Mandy will need to make sure to notify HMRC and pay on account of the CGT due within 60 days of completion of sale, as per the new regime at 5.2.

By moving in for a year, they have saved themselves nearly £17,000 in tax!

Mark and Mandy let out their old main residence, and genuinely lived in the previously let house for a year, so they are entitled to the exemptions shown above. Note also that Mark and Mandy might well have lived there for longer had it not been for Mandy having to move to follow her work: they were not occupying the property "solely to secure PPR relief".

It is essential that you actually live in a property if you are going to claim it is your main residence. If you have another property that could be regarded as your main residence as well, **do not forget to "nominate" which one is to be your main residence** for tax purposes.

Not a Real Main Residence?

Sam and Sally are in a similar situation to Mark and Mandy – they have a main residence, and they also have a let property.

They intend to sell the let property, and they have been told that if they make it their main residence before sale, they will enjoy the same tax savings that Mark and Mandy did.

Unfortunately, the let house is some 50 miles from their main residence, in a rather run-down neighbourhood, and inconvenient for commuting to work.

They get rid of the tenant, and spend a few weekends in the ex-rental property, having nominated it as their main residence (they are "in time" to make the nomination on the basis that the let property became a possible main residence only after the tenant left and it became available for them to occupy).

They do not bother to move any of their furniture or other possessions into the house, making do with the (rather dilapidated) furniture provided for the tenant when the house was let.

They do not let their former main residence, because they need it during the week, and they do not notify their bank, their employers, insurers or anyone else of their change of address. After six months of this, they sell the ex-rental property, and claim the same reliefs as Mark and Mandy.

The inspector of taxes raises an enquiry into their tax returns, and when the above facts come out, she announces that, in her opinion, their move to the ex-rental property was a sham, and it was never their residence, so none of the reliefs enjoyed by Mark and Mandy are due to Sam and Sally.

Depending on how half-hearted their occupation of the ex-rental property was, the inspector might even argue that their tax returns were incorrect because of "deliberate and concealed inaccuracy", and seek penalties based on a percentage of the tax they tried to avoid paying (or, in this case, it could even be argued, "evade" paying!).

This may seem an extreme example, but we frequently deal with clients who have previously been advised that "all you need to do is make sure the utility bills are in your name and say you were living there" ... this falls well short of the quality of occupation really required.

10 Buy to Let ("BTL")

This sector has grown hugely in the last decade or so. In this chapter we will look at the various ways that rental income can be generated from property, and the way that profits from the letting will be taxed. We will also look at the tax implications of selling your BTL property.

Clearly, this is income separate to that derived from property development itself. But it is relevant to property developers, since letting a developed property while waiting to sell (which was all too common at the onset of the global financial crisis c2008/9) will generally be subject to these rental Income Tax rules. The guidance is aimed mainly at individuals and co-owners, although many of the principles will likewise apply to corporate landlords.

10.1 Income from property

If you personally own and let property, you will be liable to Income Tax on the profit you make, after taking account of the expenses you have to pay.

Income tax is charged at the following rates for 2023/24, according to your total income for the tax year:

First £12,570	Nil (this is your "personal allowance")
Next £37,700	20% (the "basic rate")
£50,270 to £125,140	40% (the "higher rate")
Over £125,140	45% (the "additional rate")

Note that, for tax-adjusted incomes over £100,000, the personal allowance is progressively withdrawn, producing a marginal rate of tax of 60% on earned and rental incomes between £100,000 and £125,140 – by which time the Personal Allowance is completely lost. The 45% Additional Rate threshold was lowered from £150,000 to its new level as above, with effect from 6 April 2023, to apply once the Personal Allowance is 100% forfeit.

10.2 Capital v Revenue, and "Wholly and Exclusively"

These distinctions are just as relevant for a buy to let landlord as they are for a property developer – see paragraphs 7.13 and 7.14.

10.3 Allowable Expenses

If you have a buy to let property, you can deduct the following expenses from the rent you receive in order to calculate your taxable profits (assuming they pass the "wholly and exclusively" test referred to above):

- Advertising for tenants for your property – but not the cost of advertising your property for sale, as this would be a capital expense (albeit potentially deductible for CGT purposes)

- Bad debts

- Cost of providing services to tenants – for example, if you pay for the gardening, or to keep the common parts of the property clean, the cost of this can be deducted

- Interest on loans for the purposes of the business, and the cost of obtaining them – but with an important caveat that the rules for claiming interest relief on buy-to-let residential lettings have changed significantly from April 2017, with potentially far-reaching consequences for any residential landlord who has substantial borrowings or finance costs (see 10.22 / 10.23)

- Rent collection

- Staff costs

- Repairs to the let property

- Rent paid – if you are not the owner of the property, and you rent it, then sublet it

- Rates (on commercial property), Water bills, and Council Tax – but only if you pay these rather than your tenant paying them

- Insurance of the property, including for its contents, and for loss of rents

- Legal and professional fees, including accountancy compliance costs

- Travelling expenses

We need to look at some of the above expenses in more detail:

10.4 Bad Debts / The Accruals Basis (See also Cash Basis)

Strictly speaking, the accounts for your BTL business are generally prepared on the "accruals" basis (also sometimes known as the "earnings basis"). Using this method, you account for income as it "accrues" and expenditure as you "incur" it:

Accruals Basis

Dawn has a portfolio of two rental properties. She prepares the accounts for her business to 5 April each year.

The rent on her two properties is payable six monthly in advance, and during the year she puts the rent up as shown below. The tenant of property B disputes the increase, and withholds payment of the rent due on 1 July 2023 and 1 January 2024 in protest.

Months	Property A	Property B
Jan 23 to June 23 Due 1 Jan 23	600 per month	700 per month
July 23 to Dec 23 Due 1 July 23	700 per month	800 per month (unpaid at 5 April 2024)
Jan 24 to June 24 Due 1 January 24	700 per month	800 per month (unpaid at 5 April 2024)

To find the rent for property A for the year ending 5 April 2024, we need to look at the rent over the period 6 April 2023 through to 5 April 2024:

The rent for the period 1 January 2023 to 30 June 2023 was £600 x 6 = £3,600, so for the period 6 April 2023 to 30 June 2023 it was £3,600 x (86 ÷ 181) = £1,710.

For the period 1 July 2023 to 30 June 2024, the rent was £700 x 12 = £8,400, so for the period 1 July 2023 to 5 April 2024 it was £8,400 x (279 ÷ 365) = £6,420.

Using the accruals basis, the total rent for Property A for the tax year to 5 April 2024 is thus £1,710 + £6,420 = £8,130.

The cash physically received in the year to 5 April 2024 was of course

2 x 6 x £700 = £8,400.

But that was 'earned' *for* a different (albeit mostly overlapping) period: 1 July 2023 – 30 June 2024)

<u>We use the same method for property B, so we get:</u>

6 April 2023 to 30 June 2032 = £4,200 x (86 ÷ 181) = £1,995

1 July 2023 to 5 April 2024 = £9,600 x (279 ÷ 365) = £7,338 (note none of this had actually been received by 5 April 2024)

Total rent **due** for year to 5 April 2024 = £1,995 + £7,338 = £9,333

Total of rent from both properties = £17,463

17,463 is the figure to be included for rental income in Dawn's accounts under the standard Accruals basis, despite the fact that the rent on property B has not been paid for the period from 1 July 2023 to 5 April 2024.

Dawn now needs to consider if the tenant of property B will *ever* pay the rent he owes.

If Dawn has good reason to believe he will never pay her, she can claim an expense of up to £7,338 for the unpaid amount as a provision for a Bad Debt (and any legal costs to recover the debt – see 10.6) but only if there were good grounds at 5 April 2024 for believing that the rent would not be paid, and so long as it has not been paid by the time she prepares her accounts.

If a deduction is claimed for such a bad debt, and it is then recovered at a later date, the amount recovered must be treated as income received at the time the debt is paid.

The same applies to expenses:

The insurance for the two properties is paid annually in advance, on 1 August. For the period in question, the premia were:

1 August 2022 (for year to 31 July 2023) = £1,100
1 August 2023 (for year to 31 July 2024) = £ 950

For the year ending 5 April 2024, therefore, the amount to be included in the accounts for insurance is:

Period 5 April 2023 to 31 July 2023= £1,100 x (117 ÷ 365) = £353
Period 1 August 2023 to 5 April 2024 = £950 x (248 ÷ 365) = £645
Total for year to 5 April 2024 = £353 + £645 = 998

NOTE: The apportionment of expenses above has been done on a daily basis to highlight how the principle works; in practice, the 5 days in April can be ignored and the apportionment can be done on a monthly basis (i.e. for the year ending 31 March 2024 in this case), provided this is done consistently from year to year, and provided that it does not make a significant difference to the result.

Note that the traditional accruals basis risks having to recognise income due before it is actually received, while bad debts may be claimed against the missing income only where the proprietor reasonably believes that he or she will not be paid. It is, however, a more accurate approach to ascertaining one's profits or losses for a period, than simply working off cash received and paid out in a given period.

10.5 Cash Basis – You May Have to Opt Out!

The 2013 Finance Act included provision for non-corporate *traders* with turnover below the VAT registration limit (£85,000 for 2023/24) to prepare their accounts on the basis of cash received and cash spent in the period. This has effectively now been extended in the 2017 Finance Act, to cover landlords, and the main features are as follows.

Non-Corporate Landlords (including joint investors that have no companies) whose cash receipts for 2023/24 do not exceed £150,000 are **automatically in the cash basis unless they opt out**. **Landlords with incomes below that annual threshold and wishing to use the standard accruals basis will therefore need to make an election each year.**

The big advantage to cash accounting is supposedly that of simplicity: one recognises only money in, and money out, so issues like bad debts, or splitting annual insurance payments where they cover periods straddling a tax year, are avoided.

However:

- Most accountants will automatically compile accounts of rental income and expenditure on an accruals basis by default, as it is the traditional, more widely adopted, and more accurate approach

- **Most rental business income is prepaid – i.e., paid in advance. Recognising the income immediately when received will mean recognising it earlier than under the standard accruals basis, thereby accelerating the landlord's Income Tax liabilities**

- There are still special rules to deal with claiming relief for capital expenditure – unique to the cash basis

- The rules for transitioning from the accruals basis to the cash basis are complex, basically to ensure that the Crown does not lose out on tax revenue

- The rules for dealing with joint investors and/or partnerships, particularly involving spouses and civil partners, are far more involved than most people – including HMRC, based on its rather simplistic guidance – seem to realise

- There are also special rules to deal with claiming relief for finance costs such as mortgage interest (they do **not** avoid the restriction of tax relief outlined in further detail at 10.22), which broadly mimic the rules set out at 7.24 above (but on a statutory basis).

- Landlords can in some cases achieve sideways loss relief against other income, where there are Capital Allowances or certain agricultural expenses. But **loss relief against other income is prohibited under the cash basis** – see 10.19 for more on rental losses, and 12.1 for more on scenarios where Capital Allowances may be substantial.

- Where the letting is delegated to an agent, it is the agent's receipt of income and payment of expenses that determines when the landlord is deemed to have received / paid for items respectively. Given that agents often hold substantial balances on account, and may take weeks or months to actually pay over net amounts to the landlord, landlords may well still end up paying tax on significant amounts of income that they have not actually received themselves.

- The special rules for dealing with a lease premium are ignored – a landlord in the position of being able to charge a premium on a short lease might be quite disappointed to pay Income Tax rates thereon in full, instead of CGT (see 12.2)

In broad terms, where a business is receiving income in advance and is profitable, then adopting the cash basis will result in recognising income sooner, so profits will be deemed to increase for tax purposes and more tax will be payable earlier.

Landlords should speak to their Tax Adviser or accountant, about which approach – Cash or Accruals basis – should work best for them. The answer may change, from one year to the next.

Generally speaking, I would recommend that all but the very 'smallest' BTL landlords within the scope of the regime should be electing out of the cash basis, unless the pandemic (or indeed other factors) has resulted in a significant element of late-paying tenants that cannot be provided for as bad or doubtful debts.

However, if the pandemic, etc., has resulted in an unusually high level of late payment, it may be appropriate to adopt the cash basis temporarily, and then revert to the accruals basis once cashflow has recovered – and make use of the 6-year "spreading adjustment" that arises when leaving the cash basis (see, for example, the Property Income Manual at PIM1098).

Cash Basis for Property Developers - The cash basis for unincorporated trading businesses, while similar, has 2 fundamental flaws, as far as property developers are concerned, which means that very few would even consider it:

1. Interest relief is capped at no more than £500 a year, and
2. Unlike with trading losses generally, (but just as for the cash basis for landlords as set out above), losses arising on the cash basis may **not** be set against other income, or carried back against income in earlier tax years, but only carried forwards against future trading profits

10.6 Rent Collection

If you pay an agency to deal with the letting of your property, their fees are allowable, as are any similar costs associated with the collection of rent, such as the cost of suing a tenant for rent arrears.

10.7 Staff Costs

If you employ anyone to help you in your rental business, the cost of their pay is an allowable deduction, subject to the "wholly and exclusively" principle. If, for example, you employ a gardener/handyman who does work on your own home as well as on your buy-to-lets, you should apportion his pay on a reasonable basis between his work on the BTL properties (allowable as a deduction against rental income), and on your home (not allowable). Likewise employing a family member would be an allowable expense, provided the payment was commensurate with the work undertaken.

Note that you cannot claim a deduction for the time you, the landlord, spend working for your own unincorporated business.

If your property business is run through a limited company, however, the position is different and you might well want to charge a salary as a director or officer of your own company – see my guide **"How to Use Companies to Reduce Property Taxes"**, available through the Property Tax Portal.

10.8 Repairs and Renewals, and Replacing the Entirety of the Asset

This can be a minefield! The basic principle has already been explained across 7.13 – 7.15:

Repairs are revenue expenses, and allowable against income, but improvements are capital expenditure, and not allowable against income (although they may be deducted from the capital gain on disposal for CGT purposes).

The problems arise when we are at the borderline between a repair and an improvement. Perhaps the easiest way to consider the fundamental principles is to take something like a laptop computer, used in a tax consultancy business:

- If the laptop breaks and has to be completely replaced, then that is a capital item, not a repair. **I have replaced the asset in its entirety, and that is always a capital cost.**

  As an aside, I might be able to claim Capital Allowances for the cost of certain qualifying assets like a laptop or other office equipment, (see 7.17 – 7.19 above) but that is a separate tax relief, and the cost of replacing the laptop would not be allowed as a normal deduction for tax purposes in the business accounts themselves (note that the rules under the Cash Basis differ).

- Let's say instead that the problem is the graphics card and the laptop is fine once that component is replaced. This counts as a repair to the asset – the laptop – and would be allowable against business profits.

- Finally, let's say that instead of simply *replacing* the graphics card on a like-for-like basis, I decide to get a significantly superior replacement graphics card. That is an improvement to the overall asset, and will again be a capital cost that will not be allowed as a deduction in the business accounts.

The key point to bear in mind for BTL residential properties is that in most cases, where the thing being repaired or replaced is attached to the property, the "asset" in question is the overall property. Replacing a kitchen is like replacing a component (e.g., a graphics card) in a laptop, so will be a capital improvement only if the new kitchen is superior to the quality of the kitchen it replaced.

Repairs, Improvements, and "The Entirety"

Bill and Ben are both BTL landlords. Bill owns a two-bedroom house he lets out, and so does Ben. In order not to complicate this Case Study, they have both kindly agreed not to insure their properties against storm damage!

One day, a severe storm destroys the rooves of both properties.

Bill pays to have the roof replaced with a similar one – this costs him £8,000.

Ben takes the opportunity to have the loft of the house converted into a new flat, raising the height of the walls by one metre. The cost of this is £30,000.

Bill is allowed a deduction for the whole of the £8,000. He has replaced the damaged roof with a similar one, and this is a repair – the roof is not a distinct asset but part of the let property.

Ben gets no deduction at all for his £30,000. This is because the conversion of the loft is clearly an improvement, and the replacement roof is part of that improvement. He may, however, get a deduction in his CGT calculation, if and when the property is sold or otherwise disposed of. He may *potentially* be able to claim a reduced rate of VAT be charged on his builder's supplies of construction services, to reduce his project costs (including materials where applicable) – see 7.9.

This may seem unfair, but the facts in Ben's case are based on one of the leading cases on the subject of repairs *(Thomas Wilson (Keighly) Ltd v Emerson, in 1960).* Note that in some cases, it may be possible to break projects down into distinct repair and capital elements, so that the cost attributable to the repair component may be claimed as a business cost for tax purposes.

A good example might be where I replace the kitchen in my BTL property, which originally had (say) 10 units, with a similar-quality kitchen but that has 12 units: the cost of acquiring and installing the 2 extra units would be a capital improvement, while the 10 units would be a "like-for-like repair" and allowable against rental income.

10.9 "Notional Repairs"

There used to be a concession, whereby in a case like Ben's in 10.08 above, a claim would have been accepted for "notional repairs" – that is, for the cost of repairs that were no longer necessary because of the improvements. Under this concession, Ben could have been given a deduction for the £8,000 he would otherwise have had to spend on repairing the roof.

Caution: This concession was withdrawn from April 2001, and "notional repairs" can no longer be claimed in such cases.

10.10 Modern Materials

Sometimes it is almost impossible, or impractical, to repair a property by replacing "like with like" as Bill did. Perhaps the best example is double glazing. When double-glazing was first introduced to the market, it was considered to be better than standard single-glazed units in terms of heat and noise insulation. But double-glazing is now considered the "norm", and it is often more difficult / expensive to specify single-glazed units.

If your BTL property has old fashioned single-glazed windows, and these need to be replaced, it is likely to be easier and actually cheaper to install modern double glazing rather than to have replacement single-glazed windows made. In a case like this, where the "improvement" is a result of modern materials and techniques, HMRC will usually accept that the expenditure is on a repair (allowable), not an improvement.

10.11 Repairing Newly-Acquired Property

If you buy a BTL property that is in a dilapidated state, then it is possible that the cost of putting it right may be regarded as capital expenditure (in effect, part of the cost of buying the property itself) and so not be allowed as an expense against the rent.

This is likely to be the case if:

- The property was not in a fit state to be let when you bought it, so the improvements were necessary to make it possible to use it in your business in the first place, or

- The price of the property was **significantly** reduced as a result of its poor condition

In other cases, however, repairs before the first letting are an allowable expense – note that there is a common misconception – even amongst tax inspectors – that they are not allowable.

10.12 Legal and Professional Fees

Whether these are allowable depends on whether they are associated with capital or revenue expenditure.

The following legal and professional fees are capital, and so **cannot** be deducted from the rent (although some may be deductible for CGT purposes, and some would be deductible against income for a **property development** business):

- Fees relating to the purchase of the property (but in contrast would be allowable against a property *developer's* profits, as a cost of developing and then selling the property)

- Fees for drawing up an agreement relating to the first letting of a property, if the lease is for more than one year

- Fees for getting planning permission for an extension – an improvement to the property (but allowable, for property development, etc.)

- Fees relating to the sale of the rental property (but, again, allowable as a cost of selling for a property *developer*)

The following are of a revenue nature, and so can be deducted from the rent:

- Fees relating to the first letting of the property where the lease is for less than a year

- Fees connected with the **renewal** of a lease (provided it is for less than 50 years)

- Insurance valuations

- Accountancy costs for preparing rental accounts and tax computations

- Subscriptions to associations representing the interests of landlords

- The costs associated with rent reviews or arbitration

- The costs of evicting a bad tenant (if he is to be replaced with a new one, but not if the property is to be sold)

- HMRC also generally allows the cost of a **replacement** short-term lease which is on similar terms to a previous agreement on a particular property – say where a BTL property frequently changes tenants. See their Property Income Manual at PIM2120.

10.13 Furniture, etc.

In general, a landlord of furnished residential property cannot claim the standard Capital Allowances deduction for **capital expenditure**, e.g., on buying free-standing items such as:

- Cookers
- Electrical appliances
- Furniture
- Carpets and curtains
- Cutlery and crockery

This is because claims for items to be used inside a dwelling (in a property being, or to be, let out) are ineligible for Capital Allowances, although this does not prevent a BTL landlord from claiming Capital Allowances on office furniture and equipment that he or she will use in the business generally (see 10.18 below). As an alternative, the landlord used to be able to claim a "wear and tear" allowance (but see below):

10.14 Renewals Allowance 2.0 aka Replacement of Domestic Items Relief: A Lesson in Tax Legislating

It used to be possible to claim the cost of renewing, or **replacing** the sort of items listed above, albeit not the cost of buying the original items, but HMRC decided – with very little warning – to stop allowing this treatment for expenditure incurred after 5 April 2013.

There was considerable dispute from the tax profession about whether HMRC had the statutory power to abolish this Renewals Basis and, in the end, the government decided to introduce something called "Replacement of Domestic Items Relief", that looks, sounds and smells very much like the Renewals Basis they said they'd abolished. The "new" relief applies from April 2016 – **and is available only for residential lettings** – effectively to replace the old Wear and Tear Allowance (see below) and Renewals Basis – both of which were supposed to provide relief basically because residential property landlords could not claim Capital Allowances for assets in let dwellings.

Caution: NEVER TRY TO APPLY COMMON SENSE TO TAX. Tax, like the past, is a foreign country; they do things differently there!

10.15 How Replacement of Domestic Items Relief Works

You get **no** tax deduction for the cost of the original item but only for subsequent replacement(s). Of course a property may have included a cooker, fridge, etc., when it was originally acquired for the BTL business.

Where the replacement item is essentially similar to the original 'old' item, then the allowable amount is the cost of replacement. If the replacement item is superior to the original item, then you can claim only for the cost of replacing on a 'like-for-like' basis.

Incidental expenditure such as costs of removal or installation are allowed, but any proceeds from (for example) scrapping the old item should be deducted from the allowable cost of its replacement. The relief is not available for Furnished Holiday Accommodation (see Chapter 11) because Capital Allowances *can* be claimed instead.

The relief is not available for items fixed to the property, such as integrated appliances, baths, sinks, etc. But these may instead be allowable simply as a repair to the entirety of the let residential property (see 10.8 above).

Replacement of Domestic Items Relief

1: Zack replaces a washing machine in in one of his BTLs with a washer-dryer, which cost £500. A washer-only equivalent would have cost just £400, so Zack can claim only £400 on the replacement item. **Note** when Zack comes to replace the washer-dryer a few years later, then he will be able to claim the full cost of a replacement, similar-standard washer-dryer, (however much that cost is then), because he is then replacing a washer-dryer.

#2: Winona buys a fridge for £500 to replace an old fridge in her BTL property. The vendor charges her an extra £25 to dispose of the old fridge, but she gets a £100 trade-in credit directly from the manufacturer.

Like-for-like replacement	**500**
Add: cost of disposal old fridge	**25**
Less: Trade-in	**(100)**
Net Relief	**425**

10.16 Wear and Tear Allowance (up to April 2016)

Up until April 2016, a landlord of a furnished residential property could deduct 10% of the "net rent" each year. The "net rent" meant the rent receivable, less any expenses normally borne by a tenant, but borne by the landlord instead (such as council tax, broadband, water/sewage charges, and so on).

The Allowance was basically intended to meet the landlord's extra costs in providing furniture, and 10% was felt to be a reasonable approximation.

Wear and Tear Allowance (up to April 2016)

Gordon bought a BTL property and furnished it. He let it for £900 per month, and agreed that he would pay the council tax and the water rates on the property. These came to £1,400 per year.

The wear and tear allowance he could claim was £940 per year:

Gross Rents	**10,800**
Less tenant's costs paid by landlord	**(1,400)**
Net Rent	**9,400**
10% of Net Rent	**940**

Unfortunately, Wear and Tear Allowance was abolished with effect from April 2016, although it would still be possible to make a claim now if it had been omitted in a year up to 2015/16 which is under enquiry – and note that Wear and Tear was available to companies that let furnished residential property, as well as for individuals, etc., under Self-Assessment.

Going forwards, it is now possible to claim only the actual costs of replacing furniture (or repairing it), using Replacement of Domestic Items Relief, as per 10.14.

10.17 Scope of Allowances / Relief

Wear and Tear allowance was designed to cover only the sort of items provided by the landlord of a furnished letting that would normally be provided by the tenant of an unfurnished property. It did **not** cover items that were effectively part of the property, such as central heating systems, baths, washbasins, water tanks, and so on. Replacement of Domestic Items Relief follows that approach, so is not available for fixtures and fittings.

However, the cost of replacing fixtures and fittings can still potentially be claimed as a repair to the overall property as a discrete (distinct) asset, provided it does not comprise a capital improvement. Replacing fixtures such as these is considered a repair to the fabric of the building itself, just like replacing a broken window – see 10.8 Repairs and Renewals above.

10.18 Capital Allowances (CAs)

For information and worked examples covering the mechanics of Capital Allowances for cars and other assets, including the 100% initial tax deduction from the Annual Investment Allowance, please see 7.17 – 7.19.

CAs can also be claimed on other machinery and plant used for a rental business. They cannot be claimed on machinery or plant which forms part of a dwelling let as residential property, but they can be claimed on such items as:

- Cars (see 7.17)
- Office equipment and machinery used in the landlord's office(s)
- Computers used in the landlord's business
- Tools used for maintenance
- Plant in the common parts of residential property such as apartment blocks; for example lifts, security systems and central heating in the lobby, stairwell, etc. (where they are not in the dwellings themselves).

In contrast, it is often possible with **commercial** property lettings (and hotels and Furnished Holiday Lets) to claim substantial Capital Allowances on certain types of plant and machinery installed in the let building, as there is no restriction on items (such as furniture) used in the let parts of a commercial property – see 12.1 for more on CAs for commercial property. Capital Allowances cannot be claimed under the Cash Basis – see 10.5 – (with the exception of cars), although relief can sometimes be claimed for the capital cost itself.

10.19 Losses for BTL investors

10.19.1 Income Losses

Basically, all of the lettings you have in the UK are regarded as one business for the purposes of tax, so if you make a loss on one letting (perhaps because of a large repair bill), that loss can be set against your net rental income from your other properties as part of the same business. If you also have properties let overseas, then they are deemed to be in a separate business and your UK property losses cannot be set against overseas property profits (and *vice versa*)

If you have no other properties, or if there is still some loss left after setting it off against the income from them, then the remaining loss can be carried forward to the next tax year, and the next, and so on, for as long as you are a landlord, until it has been relieved against letting income.

Losses on lettings cannot normally be set against any other income of the year (such as your salary, profits from your trade or profession, or other investment income such as bank interest).

The only exception to this is where part of the loss includes Capital Allowances (or certain agricultural expenses) – that element can be set off against your other income for the year of the loss and the following year. Such claims are relatively rare for typical residential BTL businesses because Capital Allowances claims themselves tend to be quite modest, given that Capital Allowances are not available for capital items inside a normal BTL dwelling. However, commercial properties can result in much more substantial CAs claims, which can be quite useful. Another reason to eschew the cash basis for landlords is that even where losses are attributable to Capital Allowances, sideways loss relief against other income is prohibited under the cash basis.

Note that while you should pool all of your personally- and jointly-owned rental properties together, property profits and losses from acting in a 'proper' partnership or as a Trustee should be pooled separately. Likewise, losses on properties that are not let on a commercial basis – say at a significant discount to a close friend or relative – are ring-fenced and may not be deducted against mainstream letting profits. Conventional losses from an ordinary BTL business are also streamed separately from profits from Furnished Holiday Accommodation, and *vice versa* – see Chapter 11.

It is sometimes difficult to decide whether you are simply a joint or co-owner in a property letting business, or a partner in a property letting partnership, and we shall consider the main issues in the next section – see 10.20.

10.19.2 Capital Losses

If a property developer sells a property at a loss, then it is likely a loss arising to the trade of developing and selling property – an Income Tax loss (see 7.22). A property investor who sells a rental property at a loss will be subject to the CGT rules for capital losses.

Capital losses are set against capital gains arising in the same year, which may mean that a loss made by an individual (or a non-corporate body) is used against a gain that would otherwise be covered by his or her CGT Annual Exemption. This may seem unfair, but if the taxpayer ends up with a net loss, it can be carried forwards indefinitely to set against the next capital gain and will be used only to reduce aggregate gains in that later year to the point where they can then be covered by the relevant Annual Exemption, so large capital losses carried forwards will not continually be frittered away against Annual Exemptions in later years:

Example

Indra acquires 3 similar terraced properties in 2022 for £300,000 as a "job lot" at auction, with the intention of doing them up and letting them out: - he is therefore a property investor, not a trading property developer. Unfortunately, one of the properties has suffered substantial subsidence and costs spiral; he is ultimately forced to sell both the blighted property and one of the remaining two properties to recover some liquidity:

	Property 1	Property 2
Sale (2023/24)	150,000	165,000
Acquisition cost	(100,000)	(100,000)
Repair / refurbishment	(100,000)	(35,000)
Net Capital Gain/(Loss)	(50,000)	30,000
Offset In-Year Losses		(50,000)
Net Loss to Carry forwards		(20,000)

However, if Indra could stagger the disposal so that the loss on Property 1 arises in the tax year **before** the gain on Property 2:

	Property 1	Property 2
Sale (2023/24)	150,000	
Acquisition cost	(100,000)	
Repair / refurbishment	(100,000)	
Net loss carried forwards	(50,000)	
Sale (2024/25)		165,000
Acquisition cost		(100,000)
Refurbishment		(35,000)
Net gain		30,000
Deduct Annual Exemption*		(3,000)
Deduct losses b/fwds	27,000	(27,000)
Chargeable 2024/25		Nil
Losses to carry forwards	(23,000)	

By crystallising the capital loss separately in its own tax year, Indra has secured £3,000 extra to carry forwards. Whether it is 'worth it' will depend on:

- How urgently Indra needs to recover cash liquidity
- How volatile is the local housing market (there is not much point to holding out for better capital losses if the selling price of Property 2 falls by £15,000 in the interim!) and
- How likely it is that Indra will get to make substantial future capital gains, against which that enhanced capital loss might be set.

* The Annual Exemption was £12,300 in 2022/23 but is scheduled to fall to just £3,000 in 2024/25. Of course the properties might instead have been acquired through joint ownership with spouses, friends or family, in which case the overall enhancement of capital losses through staggering disposals could be significantly increased, across all the co-investors, in aggregate.

10.19.3 Lost Deposit on Off-Plan Purchases

HMRC has traditionally resisted claims for capital losses where an investor funds a deposit and/or stage payments for an off-plan development that goes wrong, broadly by arguing that the investor never actually acquired anything in the first place, then to lose.

However, a recent tax case (**Lloyd-Webber & Anor v HMRC [2019] UKFTT 717**) held that these were not (ahem), *phantom* losses, but could validly be claimed for CGT purposes: the assets might not have been tangible land or buildings but were nevertheless substantive contractual rights. This is arguably very good news for off-plan investors who suffer a loss when a deal falls through, but note:

- This was a case heard at the First-Tier Tribunal and, although persuasive, does not set a binding precedent (although the appellate case on which this judgment was based certainly did)

- The judgment implied that the Lloyd-Webbers were successful only because the *developer* had failed to complete the contract, and the outcome would likely have been different if they as *investors* had abandoned the contract instead (see also TCGA 1992 s 144, and Drake v HMRC [2022] UKFTT 00025 (TC)).

If you think that this may apply, then you should seek advice: **note that capital losses must be claimed under the Self-Assessment process, and could be permanently forfeit if they are not included in a tax return.**

10.20 "Partnerships", Couples and Joint Letting of Property

It is not unusual for there to be more than one owner of a let property. Sometimes this is described by those concerned as a "partnership", but you should be aware that HMRC take the view that in the case of a typical investment property with more than one owner, the business is a "joint venture" between joint or co-owners, rather than a partnership.

Their logic for this is that what they call the "passive" letting of property is not sufficiently "business-like" for the property owners to be "persons carrying on a business in common with a view to profit" – this is the definition of a partnership in Section 1 of the Partnership Act 1890.

Given that HMRC recognise that joint owners of property may generally agree to divide the letting profit between them in any way they choose (and not necessarily in the same proportions as their ownership of the property), this may not seem important, but in the case of a married couple or a civil partnership, there can be a problem.

Where a property is owned in joint names by a married couple or a civil partnership, the legislation requires that they be taxed on the rental profit in one of two ways:

- 50% each, regardless of their actual shares of the ownership of the property, OR

- According to their actual ownership of the property, if this is not 50:50 and they elect for this treatment by submitting a "Form 17" to HMRC

Whereas other joint owners can agree to divide the rental profits in any proportion they wish from time to time, a married couple (or civil partnership) must use one of the above two methods to apportion the income of co-owned investment property held in joint names between them. This does not have to apply to a 'proper' business partnership between spouses or civil partners, however, which may again split profits between partners as agreed at the time – even when the partners are also spouses or in a civil partnership. (See also Chapter 11 on Furnished Holiday Accommodation). Whether or not a joint investment in a property letting business will amount to a partnership will depend on the level of business activity and organisation involved. But there can be unwelcome implications to becoming a Property Investment Partnership, such as potential SDLT exposure when changing the income profit-sharing agreements, or CGT when joining a partnership.

10.21 Travelling Expenses

See also section 7.6 for additional details. BTL landlords will typically work from a home office, such that the cost of travelling from home to another place of work will be deductible. Those running larger portfolios, however, may set up separate offices away from home, in which case travelling from home to that office is likely to be considered private commuting, and not deductible.

10.22 Finance Costs for Residential Property Investors

In 2016/17, finance costs were fully deductible so long as they related to the letting business – were incurred "wholly and exclusively" for the property business (or were apportioned if appropriate). But since April 2017 (i.e., for the 2017/18 tax year and onwards) interest relief started to be disallowed, for tax purposes only – and for borrowing for residential property letting businesses only. This is nothing to do with private use, but an industry-wide crackdown on easy finance and tax relief. (Or a politically easy way to raise tax revenues, if you're cynical – I certainly am).

The government's reasoning for introducing the measure – that it was to eliminate landlords' unfair advantage against budding private homeowners – holds about as much water as my dad's string vest: I don't see the government rushing out to slap similar tax restrictions on cab drivers, hairdressers, train operators or any other of the countless businesses that 'compete' with me for private activities but expect tax relief for financing their capital expenditure. But we are where we are, nonetheless.

The key points are:

- The regime applies to all taxpayers that pay Income Tax – individuals, partners, trusts but **not** companies (which pay 19% or perhaps 25% corporation tax as a rule)
- It tries to catch any kind of financing deal, not just a simple 'mortgage'
- It tries to catch any kind of financial cost, not just 'interest'
- It applies to **residential properties** and commercial properties are ignored
- Where there are borrowings to finance both commercial and residential properties, the amount to be disallowed should be apportioned in a "just and reasonable way"
- While property *developers* are not generally caught, someone financing the development of a property with the intention of letting it out, rather than for onward sale, is subject to the new rules
- Each tax year from 2017/18 through to 2020/21, a further 25% of the landlord's finance costs was disallowed, then to be replaced by a 20% tax "credit", (strictly, a reduction in tax liability), regardless of the landlord's actual marginal tax rate

Finance Costs for Residential Property Investors

James has 4 residential BTL properties, on which he makes a total of £12,000 profits a year, net of all costs including interest. His interest-only mortgage costs him £1,000 a month. He has a job, earning £30,000 a year. His results are as follows:

(Please note: the following example uses 2016/17 rates and allowances throughout, for ease of comparison from one year to the next)

Tax Year:	**2016/17**	**2017/18**	**2018/19**	**2019/20**	**2020/21**
	£	**£**	**£**	**£**	**£**
Earnings	30,000	30,000	30,000	30,000	30,000
Net Rent after Mortgage	12,000	12,000	12,000	12,000	12,000
Add-back Rental Finance	0	3,000	6,000	9,000	12,000
Total	42,000	45,000	48,000	51,000	54,000
Tax Liability Original	6,200	7,200	8,400	9,600	10,800
Rental 20% Tax Credit	0	-600	-1,200	-1,800	-2,400
Net Tax	6,200	6,600	7,200	7,800	8,400
Tax increase on 2016/17	0	400	1,000	1,600	2,200

There is no disallowance in 2016/17

In 2017/18, when 25% of James' mortgage interest was disallowed, the deemed increase in taxable profits actually took him only partly into the Higher Rate threshold , so he paid extra tax at only 20% on some of his increased profits and 40% on the balance; where he is only paying tax on the extra profits at 20%, the 20% rental tax 'credit' is sufficient to negate the increase in tax. Where he is paying tax at 40% on the deemed additional taxable profits, however, the 20% tax credit cannot offset all of the extra tax due, so more tax is now payable.

In 2018/19, when half of James' mortgage interest is disallowed, the extra £3,000 brought into charge is already well into the 40% threshold, so the extra 20% tax 'credit' offsets only half of the additional tax – and so on through -

2019/20 (where 75% of his mortgage interest is disallowed) to -

2020/21, by which time he is paying an extra £2,200 in tax.

Once the interest disallowed means that the landlord's total income is taxable at 40%, the additional tax due is -

Disallowed interest x (40% - 20% tax 'credit') in other words, a 20% marginal rate

In the 2022 Spring Statement, the Chancellor announced that the Basic Rate of Income Tax would be reduced from 20% to 19%, from 6 April 2023. It seems quite likely that the government neither knew nor cared that the above residual tax reduction or 'credit' available for disallowed residential finance costs would also therefore fall to 19%, by reason of ITTOIA 2005 s 274AA(5). This would have further de-valued the already-limited tax relief available for residential letting finance costs, including any "stored credit" that had not already been utilised by April 2023. Thankfully, by 17 October 2022, the latest Chancellor had decided that the reduction in the Basic Rate was more of a long-term aspiration, and was postponed indefinitely.

While unincorporated property *developers* are not directly caught by the regime, they should be very careful if they develop a residential property and then decide to let it out, either because they prefer the property as a long-term investment, or because they are struggling to sell it.

If you think you may be caught by these new rules, then we strongly recommend that you speak to a tax adviser to discuss your options: it is not an exaggeration to say that there are several businesses, otherwise perfectly viable, that will not survive these new measures, simply because the tax on mortgage costs will prove too high – particularly as we face rising interest rates. Please see Chapter 8 (offsetting interest charges before 6th April 2017 and Chapter 9 (offsetting interest charges after 6th April 2017) of the book called "How to Avoid Landlord Taxes".

It is **not** simply a case of recommending incorporation as a universal solution, not least because there can be substantial tax costs – typically CGT and SDLT – to moving an existing property letting business to a corporate vehicle, and these barriers are not so easily overcome as some people – including some advisers – seem to think.

10.23 Financing the Property, Developments & Equity Release

The costs of taking out a loan to buy a rental property (such as bank fees, commissions, guarantee fees, and valuation fees for security purposes) are an allowable expense – subject to the new restrictive regime for residential property in 10.22 above.

The same applies to interest paid on such a loan, and to interest paid on other loans, overdrafts and HP agreements, provided the loan was used to buy an asset used in the business.

Where an asset is only used partly for the business, then it may be possible to claim a proportion of the interest on a loan used to buy it.

You cannot claim loan interest if you are taking advantage of the "Rent a Room" allowance that property (an allowance of £7,500 pa, or £3,750 if there is more than one person receiving rent for the property – see 8.9).

The allowability of loan interest can provide a tax efficient way of raising cash for private expenditure:

Equity Release/Refinancing

Gordon Brown owns a house that is his main residence. He bought it in 1998 for £100,000, and there is currently a mortgage outstanding on the property of £45,000.

He is offered a new job in Outer Mongolia, and decides he will let his house while he is away. The house is now worth £300,000. Gordon renegotiates the mortgage on the house to convert it to a buy to let mortgage, and borrows a further £150,000, which he uses entirely for private expenses – say, to commission a luxury yurt.

The interest on the whole of the £195,000 borrowed is an allowable deduction against the rental income, because it represents part of the cost (the market value of £300,000) of introducing the house into the business of property letting.

The same applies in the case where there is a delay between the purchase of a buy to let property and the first letting of it: it is the market value when first introduced to the rental business that determines the extent of the proprietor's capital introduced to the business.

NOTE 1: This strategy only works if the total amount borrowed is no more than the market value of the property at the time it was first let. Once the property has been let, interest on borrowing against any further increase in its market value post-introduction will be allowable only if that loan is used for a business purpose – for example, to fund the deposit on another buy to let property.

NOTE 2: This is similar to monitoring the capital account in a trading activity to ensure that it does not go overdrawn, as per 7.24. The Cash Basis for landlords (see 10.5) requires a slightly different approach as set out in the relevant legislation – very similar in principle, but not quite the same.

NOTE 3: The refinancing to release the equity does not have to be done before the property is let for the first time – it could be done at any time while the property is still let, but the limit for interest relief is the market value at the time of the first letting, not at the time of the refinancing.

NOTE 4: There can be traps for the unwary here – if for example the proprietor draws too much out of the business for living expenses, etc., then this may restrict the amount that can be withdrawn by the equity release.

NOTE 4: The **caveat** at 7.24 for current developments in relation to withdrawing capital from a business, apply here as well: the above reflects the historic context of the regime but HMRC has recently tried to apply a quite different approach, albeit in what appears (for now) to be only a relatively few cases. If contemplating significant withdrawals from the business, it is strongly recommended that you speak to your tax adviser, to ensure that you are kept abreast of any changes in this area.

11 Furnished Holiday Accommodation

This is a special type of furnished letting, and it enjoys a number of tax advantages over the ordinary letting of furnished or unfurnished residential accommodation. We will look in detail at the advantages and the rules, but in summary, the advantages are:

- Capital Allowances for furniture and machinery and plant in the property – even in the residential parts, (unlike with ordinary BTL properties – see 10.8 and 10.13) and including original items or replacements.

- The income from the property counts as "earned income" for the purposes of making pension contributions

- Because the income is treated as "earned income" in many respects, the general rule about rental investment income from property owned jointly by a married couple or civil partnership (see 10.20) does **not** apply – they can divide the rent between themselves in any proportion they decide (like a 'genuine' partnership).

- If you sell the property, it will be treated as a business asset for CGT, so you may be able to claim Entrepreneurs' Relief (Business Asset Disposal Relief), and you can claim Rollover Relief if you reinvest in another property (these reliefs will be explained later in this Chapter).

- If you make a gift of the property (to your children, for example) you can "hold over" any capital gain.

- For Inheritance Tax, the property *may* qualify as "Business Property" but only in certain circumstances (again, see later below).

11.1 So, what is "Furnished Holiday Accommodation?"

First of all, it does **not** necessarily have to be *holiday* accommodation – for example, according to the 2019/20 data released by HMRC as referred to in 1.2 above, 360 Self-Assessment taxpayers in the Stockport area claimed to have rented out Furnished Holiday Accommodation (my working theory is that they may have only *lived* in Stockport, while letting out qualifying accommodation somewhere more sanative). The tests are all to do with the type and duration of letting, and the tenants do not have to be on holiday. In practice, it is likely that most tenants will be holidaymakers, but there is no need to make sure they are on holiday during their stay!

In order to qualify as Furnished Holiday accommodation, a property must be:

- Available for short term letting (each let under 31 days) as furnished residential accommodation on a commercial basis to the public generally for at least 210 days in the year (so not offices, and no letting at a cheap rate to friends or family during this period), and

- Actually be let on these terms for at least 105 days in the year,

A typical pattern in the UK is for there to be short term lettings for the spring, summer, and early autumn months, and then for there to be a longer term "winter let" from, for example, 1 November to the end of March, but this is not a rule – the 210 days can be made up of any days in the year, as can the 105 days.

11.2 Furnished Holiday Accommodation (FHA) in the European Economic Area

Furnished Holiday Accommodation in the European Economic Area that comes within the rules set out above enjoys similar tax privileges, but is effectively treated as a separate property business from the UK holiday lets (for now, at least; how this applies outside of the UK may of course change in time, now that the UK has left the EU).

11.3 Capital Allowances

You can claim Capital Allowances on the cost of furniture and other such capital items as cookers, fridges, and so on. (You will remember that for a normal furnished letting, these could only be dealt with by using Replacement of Domestic Items Relief, or as repairs to the fabric of the building for assets that counted as fixtures and fittings – see 10.8, 10.14/10.15, above).

You can claim the "Annual Investment Allowance" of 100%, as part of your Capital Allowances claim, on up to £1million of expenditure each year on plant and machinery, and a writing down allowance at 18% per year on any balance of expenditure (6% on "integral features" such as plumbing, lighting and heating – see 7.17 *et seq.*) There was also a Super-Deduction at a rate of 130% for expenditure on qualifying brand-new assets incurred up to 31 March 2023 – buy only where made by companies (see 7.19).

Note also that the **Renewals Basis has been abolished** by statute for all businesses except ordinary furnished lettings, where it effectively 'lives on' as Replacement of Domestic Items Relief (see 10.15 *et seq.* above). Furnished Holiday Accommodation is excluded from normal furnished lettings treatment in this context, (i.e., while it used to be eligible for the Renewals Basis, it cannot access Replacement Domestic Items Relief) basically because you can claim Capital Allowances instead.

11.4 Losses

Since April 2011, losses on FHA in the UK can be set only against other UK income from UK FHA, and the same will apply to losses on EEA FHA – they can be set only against income from other EEA FHA. FHA losses cannot be set against 'ordinary' BTL property business profits and *vice versa*.

11.5 Pension Contributions

FHA income is treated as "earned income" for the purpose of making pension contributions to your pension scheme, so it ranks alongside Bed and Breakfast, hotel and property development as a trading activity, unlike normal residential and commercial letting.

In the past, ordinary landlords without a source of earned income could **not** make tax-efficient pension contributions. This is probably less problematic since the new rules for pension schemes came into effect in 2006, (which allow modest contributions of up to £3,600 gross per annum without needing relevant earnings, such as trading profits) but it can still be useful for those who want to fund pension contributions higher than that.

11.6 Profit Split for Married Couple or Civil Partnership

Because the income is "earned income" the 50:50 rule referred to above does not apply to married couples – they can basically split the rental income between them in any proportion they agree (see 10.20).

11.7 Capital Gains Tax – for Trading Entities (and FHAs)

This is where the most significant reliefs for FHA can be found, basically by virtue of an FHA letting's being treated broadly as a trading activity for tax purposes:

11.7.1 Entrepreneurs' Relief (Business Asset Disposal Relief)

This relief allows the claimant to significantly reduce the rate of CGT payable on qualifying assets. One of the key criteria for ER/BADR is that it involves 'trading assets' so ordinary BTL investment businesses are **in**eligible; however special exception is made for FHA so it can fall within scope of this valuable relief – see Chapter 13 for more information.

11.7.2 Rollover relief

If you make a capital gain when you sell certain types of eligible business asset, you can "roll over" that gain by investing in an appropriate new business asset, and FHA is one of those assets, while normal lettings are not. So, a gain on the disposal of an FHA property is potentially eligible to be rolled over depending on the nature of the asset into which the proceeds are reinvested; likewise a gain from the disposal of an eligible business asset can be rolled over into an FHA property (or both the sold and acquired assets may be FHA property).

Rollover Relief for FHA

David owns and runs a pub – he does not live on the premises, because we explained to him when he bought it that that would make this Case Study too complicated!

He decides he would like to retire and lead a quieter life, so he sells the pub for £500,000, making a capital gain of £250,000 (before Entrepreneurs' Relief or BADR – see later). If he invests his £500,000 in ordinary letting property, he will not be able to postpone the CGT of about £24,000 on his capital gain of £250,000 (we will see how this works out when we come to Entrepreneurs' Relief).

If instead he invests the £500,000 proceeds into FHA (say in three holiday cottages), he will pay no CGT, because the gain will be "rolled over" into the FHA properties. Instead of the £250,000 gain being taxed, it is deducted from the cost of the holiday cottages (for CGT purposes) so that when he comes to sell these, he can only deduct £250,000 (real cost £500,000, less gain rolled over £250,000) when he computes the gain on the holiday cottages. Rollover Relief postpones the original gain until you sell or dispose of the replacement asset. It does not get rid of the gain forever (although the gain may potentially be reinvested and postponed again, several times).

He need not invest all the sale proceeds to get some rollover relief, but some of the gain will then be taxable. If he only spends £400,000 on the new cottages, the computation will be:

Sale proceeds on pub	500,000
Less reinvested in FHAs	(400,000)
Amount not reinvested	100,000
Amount of gain not reinvested (250,000 – 150,000)	100,000

So, he will pay CGT on a gain of £100,000. It may in some cases be appropriate not to reinvest (say) £6,000, deliberately so as to use the CGT Annual Exemption. This may become more worthwhile, if there are joint owners so there are several Annual Exemptions available. Note that you do not have to isolate or trace actual funds from the sale of one eligible asset to the acquisition of another: it is sufficient merely to invest an amount of money into a qualifying asset.

There is a limited window of opportunity for reinvesting in this way. The new eligible asset must be bought during a four-year period which begins **one year before** the old eligible asset is sold, and ends **three years after it is sold.** In some circumstances, the three-year limit after the sale of the old eligible asset can be extended, but **do not rely on this without taking advice from a Tax Adviser first.**

Note 1: Because FHA is defined by how it is let, rollover relief on investing into FHA properties will at first be granted conditionally on the basis that, provided the property is in fact used as FHA and meets all the criteria, the relief will be confirmed.

Note 2: If you subsequently occupy the FHA as your home, so that when you sell it you are entitled to some measure of relief from CGT (main residence – see Chapter 8), then the held over gain will be brought back into charge.

11.7.3 Gifts of Business Assets

Many people think that gifts avoid CGT because they did not receive any money or proceeds; HMRC will be happy to inform them that this is generally **in**correct. Normally, if you make a gift of an asset, or deliberately sell it for less than its market value, you will be charged to Capital Gains Tax as if you had sold it for its market value on the day you disposed of it (with gifts between spouses and between civil partners, who are living together as a couple, being a useful exception to that rule).

This rule applies to almost all such transfers where you intend to confer some benefit to the recipient: they do not have to be relatives or otherwise connected to you for the "market value rule" to apply. If the asset is a "business asset", however, you can hold over the gain on the gift. Normal investment properties are not "business assets" for this purpose, but FHA properties are:

Hold Over for Gifts of FHA

Some years after buying the three FHA properties, David is getting on in years, and he decides he will make a **gift** of one of his holiday cottages to his daughter, Rosie.

After rollover relief across the three properties as above, the "CGT base cost" of this particular cottage is £100,000, but its market value is now £250,000. If this were not FHA, and David gave it to Rosie, he would make a capital gain on that gift of £150,000, on which he would pay CGT of about £14,000, (assuming he is still eligible for Entrepreneurs' Relief or BADR) but as it is FHA, he can "hold over" this gain.

He will pay no CGT, but Rosie's "cost" when she comes to sell will be reduced by the gain held over, so her CGT base cost will be £250,000 less £150,000 = £100,000.

In effect, Rosie acquires the asset at David's base cost: the gain on her eventual disposal will be David's postponed gain, plus the increase in value while Rosie has owned it. But, again, she may well be able to hold over any gain on her eventual disposal, if the property in her ownership still continues to qualify as FHA – or she may plump for Entrepreneurs' Relief (Business Asset Disposal Relief – see Chapter 13).

12 Commercial Property

By "commercial property", we mean any property which is not residential property so, for example, offices, factories, shops, and warehouses would all qualify.

Most of what has been said so far about letting residential property applies to commercial property as well, but there are a few other points to bear in mind:

12.1 Capital Allowances – Don't Miss Out!

Unlike ordinary residential lettings, (excluding FHA, hotels and similar businesses), the landlord of a commercial property can claim Capital Allowances on the cost of plant and machinery in the premises he lets out. This can include:

- Heating / air conditioning
- Lifts
- Lighting and other electrical wiring
- Telecommunications and data infrastructure
- Washroom fittings, water supply, plumbing, etc.
- Kitchen fittings

It is often possible to claim a very substantial proportion of the cost of a commercial building – even one that has been held for a number of years – under the CAs rules. However, this is a very complicated and technical area, and you should take advice from a Tax Adviser if you are going to be incurring significant expenditure of this type.

In particular, if you are contemplating the purchase of a commercial property, you <u>must</u> take advice and factor Capital Allowances into your negotiations with the vendor. If you do not, you may not only miss out on some very valuable tax reliefs yourself but you could "taint" the property for any future buyers as well.

The new Structures and Building Allowance (SBA – see 7.19) should also offer buyers further useful relief on the value attributable to the 'new' construction cost of the commercial property, albeit over 33 years (3% on qualifying cost in a straight line). This is complementary to Capital Allowances.

12.2 Premia for Leases

The rules for premia apply to any lease of a property, but as they are more common in letting commercial property, I will deal with them here.

This is another highly technical area of tax, so what follows is only a very broad outline of the basic concept. If you are going to charge a premium for a lease, take advice!

A premium is a *capital* sum paid to the landlord in exchange for the landlord granting a lease to a tenant. Because capital gains are (generally) taxed at lower rates than income, it might be an attractive idea for a landlord to grant a lease at a very low rent, but with a high initial premium.

You would pay CGT on granting the premium, but there are various tax reliefs that could reduce the tax you paid to much less than the amount of the income tax you would have paid on the rent. For this reason, there are special rules for premia paid for the grant of a "short" new lease (of 50 years or less):

Premium for "Short" Lease

Aladdin has a warehouse to let, and Sinbad wants to lease it for 20 years. They agree that the rent will be £5,000 per year, and that Sinbad will pay Aladdin a premium of £30,000 on the day the lease is signed.

Because the lease is not for a period of more than 50 years, part of this premium will be treated as if it were rent paid by Sinbad, rather than a capital sum.

To find the amount, we use a percentage found as follows:

Deduct one year from the length of the lease: 20 - 1 = 19.

Multiply the result by 2: 19 x 2 = 38

38% of the premium will be treated as a capital payment.

This means that £30,000 x 38% = £11,400 will be included in a CGT calculation for Aladdin.

The remaining 62% of the premium will be treated as if Aladdin had received that much rent on the day he granted the lease to Sinbad.

62% of £30,000 = £18,600, so for the first year of letting, Aladdin's rental income from the warehouse (assuming the lease was signed on 6 April), will be rent of £5,000, plus deemed rent of £18,600 = £23,600.

From Sinbad's perspective, he can claim a deduction (if he is using the warehouse for a trade or similar) of the actual rent he pays (£5,000), plus the part of the premium treated as rent, spread over the length of his lease (£18,600 divided by 20 = £930 per year).

Sinbad is effectively getting Income Tax relief on the amount of the premium treated as Aladdin's income but Aladdin is taxed on the deemed income immediately, while Sinbad's tax relief is stretched over the life of the lease.

So, the premium has worked to turn some of the lessor's receipt into a capital gain, and only some of the payment into a deductible amount for the tenant. Note that the rules also differ for businesses applying the Cash Basis (see 10.5).

The taxation of premia is highly technical, and there are many pitfalls – for example, suppose that Aladdin's warehouse was too small for Sinbad, and they agreed that instead of paying a lump sum, Sinbad would pay for building an extension to it. This could be treated as a deemed premium, and Aladdin would be treated as if he had received a premium equal to the **increase in the market value of the property** (not simply the cost of the work to Sinbad) to Aladdin on the day the lease was signed.

We repeat: ask a Tax Adviser if you are getting involved with premia for leases!

13 Entrepreneurs' Relief (Business Asset Disposal Relief) and Investors' Relief

Entrepreneurs' Relief (ER) was introduced with effect from 6 April 2008, to replace the previous Taper Relief. It became "Business Asset Disposal Relief" ("BADR") with effect from 6 April 2020, but is commonly referred to still as Entrepreneurs' Relief.

Investors' Relief was introduced in the 2016 Finance Act, effectively as an extension to ER/BADR, but aimed more at arm's length subscribers for shares in qualifying companies – people who do **not** intend to become involved with running the company.

ER/BADR now has a cumulative Lifetime Allowance which taxes the first £1 million of eligible capital gains at a rate of only 10% instead of the usual 28% (or 20% since April 2016, basically for anything which is **not** residential property). The Lifetime Allowance used to be £10million for disposals prior to 11 March 2020, but was significantly curtailed as part of the re-launch as BADR.

The more recent Investors' Relief still has a £10million cumulative Lifetime Allowance, and works in a similar way (the Lifetime Allowance for Investors' Relief has **not** been affected by the introduction of BADR).

These reliefs are arguably of only limited relevance to property investors and unincorporated (non-limited company) developers, because they apply only to "Business Assets" – broadly, assets used for your trade, or shares in a qualifying trading company, that you have held for at least 2 years.

Aside from Furnished Holiday Accommodation, BTL businesses do not normally qualify as trading businesses, and, unless you are really quite a 'large' unincorporated property developer, most of the value of your business is likely to be found in your trading stock – selling *that* is a trading profit, not a capital gain. You could still see capital gains eligible for Entrepreneurs' Relief on the sale of any trading premises, and/or goodwill, however.

Investors' Relief is likewise available only in relation to new shares issued – a subscription – in a qualifying trading company.

The types of asset that will likely be of interest to the readers of this book which may qualify are:

- Furnished Holiday Accommodation (see Chapter 11) – though unless you are selling all of your FHA properties as a "job lot", you will need basically to show that what you are selling is capable of standing on its own two feet as a "part of a business". This can lead to highly technical arguments with HMRC, and expert advice is strongly recommended.
- Shares in a property development company (or an FHA company) – provided either:

    - You have owned the shares for at least **two** years, (for disposals prior to 6 April 2019, the minimum holding period for eligible business assets was just one year), you are a director or employee of the company, and own at least 5% of the voting shares, profits and rights to proceeds on a winding up (Entrepreneurs' Relief/BADR), or

- You have subscribed for **any** number of shares **issued** to you on or after 17 March 2016 and (will) have held them continuously for at least **three** years since 6 April 2016. (Investors' Relief – but this time, being a director or employee could disqualify the tax break, because Investors' Relief is aimed at passive investors who are **not** involved with the day-to-day running of the company).

Business Asset Disposal Relief (Entrepreneurs' Relief)

Let's say that Rosie from 11.7.3 above sells her single FHA property a few years later in 2023/24 for £500,000. The property was worth £250,000 when David gave it to her, so Rosie's own gain might seem to be just £250,000, but the value has to be adjusted for the Gift of Business Assets claim made at the time of the gift to her.

The property has qualified as an FHA throughout.

Rosie has not yet used any of her BADR Cumulative Lifetime Allowance, so at this point, up to £1,000,000 can benefit from BADR:

Capital Gains Tax		
Proceeds		500,000
Cost on Acquisition:		
Value on Transfer	250,000	
Less: Gain held over by David as Business Asset on transfer *to* Rosie	(150,000)	
		(100,000)
Taxable Gain:		400,000
Less: Annual Exemption (2023/24)		(6,000)
		394,00
Business Asset Disposal Relief (taxable @ 10%)		
Total CGT Payable:		**39,400**

If Rosie were ***in***eligible for ER/BADR, then the gain could have been taxable at 28%, and cost a further c£70,000.

Looking forwards, Rosie has £600,000 of her Lifetime Allowance available for future disposals, having used up £400,000 here, out of her £1million cumulative total that was available originally.

14 Stamp Duty Land Tax (LBTT in Scotland, LTT in Wales)

Please Note: the following is intended to be a gentle introduction to the principles of "stamp taxes" and their newly-devolved equivalents, and to give an idea of the kind of issues that property businesses might commonly encounter. For example, SDLT, LBTT and LTT each have *similar* provision for the simultaneous acquisition of multiple dwellings, and for treating the simultaneous acquisition of 6 or more dwellings as being "non-residential", (as set out below), but that does **not** mean that the mechanism works in exactly the same way in the detail – always check how the stamp tax regime applies in your region before buying!

Stamp Duty used to be part of everyone's life.

If you have an old (pre-1960) pack of playing cards, you will find that there is a "stamp" on the Ace of Spades, certifying that Stamp Duty has been paid. Certain legal documents – such as receipts – had to be signed over a Stamp – literally, over a postage stamp – and such things as medicine bottles, perfume, hats, and gloves all bore Stamp Duty. Stamp Duty was introduced by William and Mary in 1694, as a temporary tax to pay for the war against France ("to pay for the war" is a common excuse for new taxes – Income Tax was introduced in 1799, as another temporary tax, to pay for the Napoleonic War).

These days, Stamp Duty itself basically applies only to sales of shares, at a rate of 0.5% on the amount paid.

Stamp Duty Land Tax (SDLT) was introduced in 2003, and as the name implies, it is a tax on land transactions. SDLT is a self-assessed tax and, for transactions with an effective date on or after 1 March 2019, the purchaser has only 14 days to file and pay their SDLT transaction return (generally online, and usually handled by their conveyancing solicitor)

The rate depends on the amount paid for the property, and whether it is "residential" or not. 2016 saw some major changes:

- A second, higher, tier of rates for residential properties – the 3% addition
- Commercial (non-residential) properties charged on a progressive scale, rather than on an "all-or-nothing" or "slab" basis. (This follows residential property, which moved to the progressive basis in December 2014)
- However, the "sting in the tail" for commercial properties is the introduction of another higher rate for more expensive properties/transactions

Aside from temporary pandemic measures, (see earlier versions of this book), Budget 2021 also confirmed a further 2% supplement for non-residents acquiring residential property in England and Northern Ireland from 1 April 2021.

SDLT is payable by the purchaser of the property concerned, so it will be a cost for both buy-to-let landlords and property developers.

For the landlord, it is part of the cost of acquiring the property for CGT purposes, so when he or she comes to sell it, it will form part of the cost deductible to arrive at the capital gain. For the property developer, it is part of the cost of his or her trading stock.

14.1 Residential Properties

For residential property, and since 4 December 2014, SDLT has been charged at progressively higher rates in bands, rather like Income Tax, so *usually** for a home costing £260,000, the first £125,000 suffers no SDLT, the next £125,000 is taxed at 2%, and the remaining £10,000 is taxed at 5%, giving a total SDLT payable of £3,000, as set out in the "Residential Property" column in the table below.

Unfortunately, as a residential property developer, (or even a simple residential property investor), you will now be more interested in the "Higher Rate" column, introduced for purchases completed from 1 April 2016. A 3% 'surcharge' has now been introduced across all bands. While individuals may **replace** their main residence and pay SDLT at the lower rate, companies (and developers who are individuals/partners and who already have a main residence) will now have to pay SDLT at the higher rate(s):

Band	Residential Property	Residential Property – Higher Rate (+3%)
0 - £125,000	Nil	3%
£125,001 - £250,000	2%	5%
£250,001 - £925,000	5%	8%
£925,001 - £1,500,000	10%	13%
Over £1,500,000	12%	15%

*Chancellor Kwarteng's "Growth Plan" of 23 September 2022 announced an increase in the 0% starting rate band that was *supposed* to be permanent; however, Chancellor Hunt's Autumn Statement of 17 November 2022 said that this would now be a **temporary measure, applying up to 31 March 2025**:

Purchase price, etc. – Residential Properties	SDLT Rate for purchases effective 23/09/22 to 31/03/25	SDLT Rate for purchases effective prior to 23/09/22 (and post-31/03/25)	Higher Rate on Additional Dwellings (HRAD)*
Up to £125,000	**0%**	0%	**+3%**
The next £125,000 (the portion from £125,001 to £250,000)		2%	**+3%**
The next £675,000 (the portion from £250,001 to £925,000)	**5%**	5%	**+3%**
The next £575,000 (the portion from	**10%**	10%	**+3%**

Purchase price, etc. – Residential Properties	SDLT Rate for purchases effective 23/09/22 to 31/03/25	SDLT Rate for purchases effective prior to 23/09/22 (and post-31/03/25)	Higher Rate on Additional Dwellings (HRAD)*
£925,001 to £1.5 million)			
The remaining amount (the portion above £1.5 million)	**12%**	12%	**+3%**

Note:

Transactions under £40,000 consideration are basically not returnable to HMRC and are not subject to the higher rate.

There is a special relief for "First Time Buyers" that significantly extends the effective starting band(s) but this has been ignored here, on the basis that readers will almost certainly be serial property investors, ineligible to be considered "First Time Buyers".

The basic approach to whether or not the additional 3% charge is due, is to ask 2 questions:

(1) On the day of completing the purchase of your new residential property, do you now own more than one dwelling?
(2) If yes, then is your new residential property replacing your main residence?

If not, then the 3% / higher rates are due.

Note that generally, where there are several co-buyers or joint investors, it takes only one buyer to be liable to the additional 3% rate, for **the entire consideration** to be subject to the 'surcharge' – effectively, all buyers then suffer the 3% additional rate

Companies are always exposed to the Higher Rate, as they cannot be acquiring or replacing their main residence, as companies cannot have a main residence!

14.2 Mitigating the New Higher Rate(s) - Multiple Properties

There are two tax-saving devices open to those looking to acquire several residential properties in one 'job lot' – or perhaps to incorporate their existing business – where SDLT may also be in point.

14.2.1 Multiple Dwellings Relief (MDR)

This is a relief available where a taxpayer buys several dwellings at once. **SDLT is generally charged on the total consideration paid** across all properties and using the above bands, but MDR allows the buyer to apply the rate corresponding to the *average* price of a residence in a transaction – noting that the minimum rate under MDR is now effectively 3% (since the higher rates will apply – see the right-most columns in the above tables).

A single physical property may contain several "dwellings" (such as an apartment block), but advice should always be sought to ensure that MDR is correctly applied. There have been quite a few MDR cases heard at tribunal over the last few years, typically where the taxpayers have tried to claim MDR on a valuable main home that includes a modest annexe or similar, in the hope that MDR will significantly reduce the average effective rates of SDLT charged on the total consideration.

For example, Merchant & Gater v HMRC [2020] UKFTT 0299 (TC) involved an annexe (or basement, according to HMRC) that was accessible only through a shared hallway, and which the Tribunal found to be unsuitable for use by two separate households as two separate dwellings.

In Fiander and Brower v HMRC [2021] UKUT 0156 (TCC), an annexe to the main house was held **not** to be a dwelling separate to the main house, but part of the single dwelling. Critically, the annexe was **not** manifestly separated from the main house, and was incapable of being physically secured (or privately enjoyed separately) from the main house at the point of purchase. This case carries more weight as it was heard at the Upper Tribunal; the taxpayers may well rue that the previous owners had not installed a serviceable door of suitable heft or similar, to the corridor adjoining the two parts of the property in question, prior to marketing the property for sale.

Despite winning most of the MDR cases at Tribunal that have been published recently, HMRC does seem to be quite concerned at the number of claims it dislikes – leading one potentially to infer that perhaps there are many more claims that HMRC decided not to take so far. At the time of writing, HMRC is (still!) in the process of ruminating on a 2021 consultation on reforming MDR to discourage 'marginal claims', perhaps by requiring a minimum of three dwellings, or by insisting that the value attributable to any annexe comprise at least a third of the total purchase price. But it seems that the mischief largely centres around private homeowners, and any changes should not trouble property developers or investors overmuch.

14.2.2 Mixed / Six-Plus Acquisitions

Aside from MDR above, if a transaction involves either:

- "Mixed use" property, with both residential and non-residential elements, or
- 6 or more separate dwellings

Then the potentially lower "non-residential property" rates may be used (Finance Act 2003 s 116 (7)). (See Case Study at 14.4 below for a worked example).

Here again, the difference in the overall SDLT cost depending on whether the property/ies are treated as purely residential, as against mixed use/commercial, has placed some strain on the legislation and its interpretation, and HMRC's becoming increasingly concerned that it is not being used "as intended" (or, more accurately, that the relief is not being used as HMRC *thinks* it is supposed to be used).

This time, the issue tends to orient around the issue of a house's "garden or grounds", and whether or not they are truly residential, or might serve some other purpose such as grazing, agriculture or small business, such that the overall acquisition might be considered to be mixed use, and eligible for substantially lower SDLT rates. Note that the higher, residential property rates are supposed to apply only where the acquisition involves exclusively residential property (but see next).

Readers might appreciate the irony that, when HMRC is policing "garden or grounds" in the context of CGT and PPR relief for the disposal of one's main residence, taxpayers face an uphill struggle to convince HMRC that anything exceeding the statutory 0.5 hectares is *really* necessary for a home (see 8.3) but when a taxpayer wants to claim that a plot amounts to more than just "garden or grounds" in terms of SDLT, HMRC sees almost no limit to the rolling expanse that a homeowner might conceivably wish to enjoy... but remain wholly residential. To HMRC's credit the separate legislative provisions do not, alas, support the consistent treatment that taxpayers might feel they deserve.

Despite the difference in the legislation between SDLT and CGT, and stretching perhaps beyond irony and into farce, HMRC nevertheless seemed quite happy to use practically the same guidance in its SDLT manual for what constitutes "garden or grounds", as it provided for CGT – *for sixteen years* – until taxpayers actually sought to rely on it and claim the commercial SDLT rates, as the several taxpayers ultimately participating in Hyman and others v HMRC [2022] EWCA Civ 185 found to their significant cost.

Rather than being embarrassed, HMRC has doubled down and its current consultation on Multiple Dwellings Relief as at 14.2.1 above also incorporates proposals to require a minimum threshold of non-residential use before an acquisition involving residential property might be considered **not** to be exclusively residential – which might seem illogical, given the way the legislation is supposed to work, but is nonetheless accurate.

14.3 Other Reliefs

There are several other SDLT reliefs that might conceivably apply to a property development project, including where:

- An employer buys one of its employee's main/only residence if he or she is required to relocate
- A developer acquires a buyer's "old" main/only residence in exchange for one of the developer's new properties
- A Compulsory Purchase of a property, wherein the Local Authority will acquire and then sell on to the developer (but note the relief is actually claimable by the Local Authority); or where the developer has planning obligations to a Local Authority, such as to build and hand over a new play centre as part of a larger development (in which case the developer gets to claim on the initial acquisition).

14.4 Commercial (Non/Residential) Properties

For non-residential property, (which includes commercial or mixed-use properties), the 2016 Finance Act introduced from March 2016 a similar banded "progressive tax" regime to that adopted for residential property in December 2014, to replace the old "slab" approach, for freehold purchases and lease premium payments, as follows:

Non- Residential Property	Rate
0 - £150,000	Nil
£150,001 - £250,000	2%
£250,001 +	5%

In the case of other leases, the amount payable depends on the "Net Present Value" of the rent under the lease – this is a complicated calculation, best left to a tax adviser, or the HMRC website offers a "calculator" to work it out. Having established the Net Present Value, it is chargeable at:

Non- Residential Property Lease NPV	Rate
0 - £150,000	Nil
£150,001 – £5,000,000	1%
£5,000,001+	2%

Despite moving from the antiquated 'slab' system, (that applied the specified SDLT rate to the *total* consideration), the overall effect of the changes to SDLT on commercial property announced in Budget 2016 was to **increase** the aggregate SDLT yield to the Treasury: the cost will fall for lower-value commercial properties – favouring smaller businesses – but tends to rise for higher-value properties, because of the 1% rate increase on higher-value property falling in the top band.

Case Study – Multiple Residential Properties: MDR or Commercial Route?

Portia purchases 10 additional residential properties in one transaction, for a total of £3 million. The average purchase price is therefore £300,000. She is purchasing at least 6 residential properties in the same transaction, so she can choose whether to claim multiple dwellings relief, or apply the non-residential rates.

Multiple Dwellings Relief: ***Using Current Temporary Rates (to 31 March 2025)***

The SDLT due, using the higher rates (+3%) on the average purchase price of £300,000, is £11,500. This is then multiplied by the number of properties (10) to give the total amount of SDLT due - £115,000.

£0 - £250,000 @ (0% + 3%HRAD) = £7,500
£250,001- £300,000 = £50,000 @ (5% + 3%HRAD) = £4,000

Total = £11,500 for average property price of £300,000

10 property x £11,500 = £115,000

While the temporary reduction in starting residential SDLT rates applies, this makes the MDR approach particularly attractive, as it is based on the average property price.

Multiple Dwellings Relief: <u>Standard Rates</u> (pre-23/09/2022; post-31/03/2025)

The SDLT due, using the higher rates (+3%) on the average purchase price of £300,000, is £14,000. (This would have cost just £5,000 per property before the new higher rate residential bands were introduced in December 2014). This is then multiplied by the number of properties (10) to give the total amount of SDLT due - £140,000.

£0 - £125,000 @ (0% + 3%HRAD) = £3,750
£125,001 - £250,000 = £125,000 (2% + 3%HRAD) = £6,250
£250,001 - £300,000 = £50,000 @ (5% + 3%HRAD) = £4,000

Total = £14,000 for average property price of £300,000

10 property x £14,000 = £140,000

OR:

Non-Residential Rates:
The non-residential rates apply to the total transaction value – £3 million – as is the usual approach when not making a claim for Multiple Dwellings Relief. Thanks to the recent hike in non-residential rates as well, from March 2016, this will now cost £139,500.

£0 - £150,000 @ 0% = £Nil
£150,001- £250,000 = £100,000 @ 2% = £2,000
£250,001- £3,000,000 = £2,750,000 @ 5% = £137,500

Total = £139,500

During the period of the temporary reduction in the starting residential SDLT rates applicable for purchases up to 31 March 2025, Portia will save £24,500 by choosing the Multiple Dwellings Relief option. (But if comparing the non-residential route to the standard residential rates as will apply again for purchases from 1 April 2025, Portia would save herself £500 using non-residential rates, as against Multiple Dwellings Relief.)

While the average property price is low, the total SDLT due per residential property can be significantly less in aggregate than the lump sum due as if for commercial properties, in which case the Multiple Dwellings Relief route will typically offer the greater saving. But if the average price of the dwellings starts to rise, then the more expensive higher residential rates will likely push Portia more towards adopting the mixed/commercial rates, where the maximum rate is "only" 5%.

In the absence of either treatment, however – if Portia were to apply the default residential rates table to the **total** consideration (see also 14.9) – then she would be looking at a total SDLT bill of £361,250 (or £363,750, if acquired after 31 March 2025, when the temporary reduction in starting rates is scheduled to finish).

14.5 "Chargeable Consideration"

SDLT is based on the "chargeable consideration" paid for the property, so in the case of a gift for no consideration, no SDLT should normally be payable, though there are some notable exceptions to this:

14.6 Debts (Including Mortgages)

If you make a gift of an interest in property which has a loan secured on it, the person receiving the gift may assume at least partial/joint responsibility for the mortgage (the lender may even insist on it). If you make a gift of a third of the property, then for SDLT purposes, one third of the mortgage will be deemed to be "chargeable consideration" that has been "paid" by the recipient:

Gifts and SDLT

David owns an investment property valued at £300,000, on which there is a mortgage of £200,000. He makes a gift of a half share in the house to his wife, Eileen. They also own their own home. The lender insists that Eileen be added to the list of mortgagors, (borrowers), so that she is jointly and severally liable for the mortgage debt. This means that, in theory, she could ultimately be liable for 100% of the mortgage - £200,000.

The "Chargeable Consideration" for this transaction is nevertheless £100,000 (half the mortgage, because Eileen has acquired half the interest in the property, regardless of how much debt she has actually agreed to take on). This is chargeable at 3%, using the higher rates applicable to residential properties. (A married couple may have only one main residence, so this must also be an additional residence for Eileen).

14.7 Transfer to a Company

Where a property is transferred to a company, and either:

- The person making the transfer and the company are "connected", OR
- The company issues any shares in exchange for the property transferred

Then the company must pay SDLT on the **market value** of the property – even if the land is transferred by way of a gift for no consideration. See also 14.100 for more on corporate acquisitions.

14.8 Exchange of Property

Sometimes one property is exchanged for another, with either no cash changing hands, or with one side paying "equality money".

Exchange of Property

Mrs Time owns one home worth £210,000 and Mrs Chance (no relation) owns one home worth £260,000. They agree to exchange homes, with Mrs Time paying Mrs Chance £50,000 "equality money".

Under the temporary starting rates in force for residential purchases up until 31 March 2025, Mrs. Time's consideration of £260,000 – being her house, worth £210,000, plus cash of £50,000 – will be £500. Under the standard rates (to which we shall revert from 1 April 2025) the SDLT charge would be £3,000.

Mrs Chance is deemed to have given chargeable consideration of £210,000, made up of her house worth £260,000 LESS the £50,000 paid to her by Mrs Time. Under the temporary rates, her SDLT charge will be £nil (it is less than £250,000) but if the exchange were to take place after 31 March 2025, it would be £1,700.

The SDLT would be more – using the higher rates – if they were not exchanging their main home but a rental or development property instead.

14.9 "Linked Transactions"

Where two or more transactions are "linked", SDLT is charged on the rate applicable to the total consideration involved.

Transactions are "linked" if they are part of the same scheme, arrangement or series of transactions between the same vendor and purchaser, or persons "connected" with them.

Sale of House and Garden

Mr and Mrs Meadowcroft want to buy a house from Mr Smart. The price is £290,000, which means SDLT of £2,000 (they are replacing their main home, so use the lower residential SDLT rates; it would be £4,500 if purchased after 31 March 2025).

Mr Smart suggests that if Mr Meadowcroft bought the house for £250,000, and Mrs Meadowcroft bought the garden for (say) £39,995, Mr Meadowcroft would currently pay £nil SDLT, and Mrs Meadowcroft would not even have to make an SDLT return – see 14.1 (again, for a purchase after 31 March 2025, Mr. Meadowcroft's proposed liability would be £2,500 on a payment of £250,000).

Unfortunately, this will not work – because Mr and Mrs Meadowcroft are "connected" (being husband and wife), the two transactions are "linked", and so they will pay SDLT of £2,000 on the aggregate consideration paid between them.

14.10 Companies, Stamp Taxes and ATED

In the past, companies holding properties were seen as a convenient way of transferring ownership of a property without actually having to sell the property itself and potentially triggering an SDLT charge on the buyer: one could simply sell or transfer the shares in the company instead. Various anti-avoidance measures have been introduced to make this less attractive, and notably, now:

1. Where a company buys any number of single dwellings whose individual **value** exceeds £500,000, (a so-called "high value dwelling"), then a flat rate or "slab" 15% SDLT charge may apply, which could in theory be supplemented by the 2% surcharge for non-resident acquisitions.
   There are numerous exceptions to this, notably, where the property is bought:

   - To be used in a property rental business, operated on a commercial basis with a view to a profit
   - By a property developer / trader as stock, for refurbishment or development, and re-sale
   - When acting as bare Trustee for individuals (i.e., the company is the legal owner, and has no equitable or beneficial interest in the property, so for tax purposes, the "owner" is the individual(s)
   - To be occupied by an employee of the company (although a taxable "benefit in kind" Income Tax charge may well be assessable on the employee for the provision of living accommodation)

     Note, however, that occupation of such a residence by a shareholder of the company, (or a relative, etc.), **even if under tenancy on arm's length commercial terms**, can result in the withdrawal of the relief and the 15% slab rate being charged.

2. An Annual Tax on such high-value "Enveloped Dwellings", (ATED), as follows for 2023/24 rates:

Dwelling Property Value	ATED Charge (£)
£500,001 - £1,000,000	4,150
£1,000,001 - £2,000,000	8,450
£2,000,0001 - £5,000,000	28,650
£5,000,001 - £10,000,000	67,050
£10,000,001 - £20,000,000	134,550
£20,000,0001+	269,450

   As with the slab 15% SDLT charge on the purchase of one or more "high-value residential properties" above, there are exceptions to the ATED charge, such as where the property is let out as part of a property rental business, or where the property is being developed, etc., but note that the **relief from ATED must be claimed on an annual basis** and that, again, occupation by a shareholder, or a relative, etc., can negate the relief from charge.

   Property letting companies dealing with such high value residential properties need also to monitor any significant "void periods" and to keep good contemporaneous records to rebut any assertion by HMRC that the property is no longer being let out on a commercial basis, etc.

The key point to take away from these measures is to keep an awareness that, if your company is going to acquire residential property valued at £500,000 or more (or, in the case of ATED, if your company will end up owning a residential property that is worth more than £500,000 ***or may become worth more than £500,000 at some point in the future***), then take professional advice to ensure that you are not caught out by these charges.

Finally, as mentioned at the beginning of this Chapter, the details as set out above are representative for England and Northern Ireland and the equivalent rules in Scotland and now Wales, while similar, are NOT the same – for example, the Scottish "Additional Dwelling Supplement" that covers scenarios where, as a BTL investor, you are **not** simply buying or replacing your own home, rose to 6% from 16 December 2022, which is double the 3% additional rate in England and Northern Ireland: **always check how the regime applies in your region before buying!**

15 Tax Investigations

HMRC have the power to "enquire" into any tax return from a company, a partnership, or an individual. They do not have to give a reason for the enquiry.

Anyone in the property business may face an Enquiry – a certain number of random Enquiries are opened every year.

Enquiries come in different forms:

"Aspect" Enquiries. These are the least serious type of Enquiry – though they have been known to develop into Full Enquiries as they progress. In an Aspect Enquiry, the inspector will ask questions about a specific issue in the return – a favourite example for a property *letting* business would be to check if amounts claimed for repairs to a let property are in fact capital improvements (that cannot be deducted from rental income). A common query for property *developers* would be whether or not projects in progress at the accounts year-end had been correctly valued, so as to recognise an appropriate level of profit on sales made in the year.

Many Aspect Enquiries are closed down with no penalties being charged – though this is not always the case if large or blatant errors are found – but there will be interest to pay on any additional tax that is collected, running from the date the tax would have been paid if the return had been correct in the first place.

"Compliance Visits". These are aimed at checking that the business has complied with its obligations under the various laws and regulations it is obliged to obey. A compliance visit can be arranged to check that you are keeping the appropriate business records generally, but most are more focused on particular aspects of tax compliance. For property businesses, the commonest are:

- **Construction Industry Scheme (CIS) compliance**
  The CIS applies to all property developers (but not normally to property investors), and requires them to check the credentials of all the subcontractors they use, such as plasterers or electricians who are in business on their own account, and to record and report all payments to them, while in some cases deducting tax from those payments and accounting for that tax to HMRC directly (see 7.7 – 7.8 above).

- **PAYE and benefits in kind**
  A sole trader or partnership will only be liable to this type of Enquiry if it has employees – but it is possible that people treated as self-employed sub-contractors should instead be categorised as employees, as we saw earlier, so it can happen that a CIS Compliance Visit also takes in PAYE compliance. The Enquiry will check if the business has operated PAYE correctly, and if all benefits in kind and expenses payments have been correctly reported on the annual Forms P11D. Limited companies may have only one or two director/shareholders, but directors are subject to PAYE for any salary, bonuses or benefits in kind, so any limited company may be a target for a PAYE visit. See also 7.20– 7.21 above.

- **VAT**
  HMRC will (for example) check that any property purchases have been handled correctly where there are Transfer of a Going Concern issues, and that any options to tax on commercial buildings have been put in place properly. Also, where the business has applied reduced rates of VAT, such as on change of

use, HMRC will want to check the validity of the basis for the claim. A business that is "partially exempt" (see 7.9) may well receive the occasional VAT visit.

"Full" Enquiry. This is the type of Enquiry that is generally referred to as a Tax Investigation, and it will involve the inspector looking at all the business accounts and records, and in some cases the private bank statements, etc., of the proprietors. It may also involve some or all of the more specialised types of Enquiry referred to above.

This is not the place for a detailed examination of how to deal with a tax investigation, but there is one vital piece of advice – **do not attempt to deal with it yourself!** In particular, if you receive a notice from the tax inspector to say he has decided to "Enquire" into your return, **seek professional help immediately** – in the first instance, from your accountant, though in serious cases he may well want to call in tax specialists like us.

If it is found that tax has been underpaid, then penalties may be due.

There is one other kind of investigation to consider.

This is where HMRC believe there has been serious tax fraud. In these cases, they will send you a "Contractual Disclosure Form" under Code of Practice 9 ("COP 9"). If you are ever sent a CDF, it is ABSOLUTELY ESSENTIAL to take expert advice from a suitably experienced Tax Adviser **immediately**.

UNDER NO CIRCUMSTANCES try to handle this yourself, and, at the risk of offending the profession, it is unlikely that your regular accountant will have the expertise to deal with a CDF investigation.

To end this part, here are the golden rules for dealing with tax enquiries:

- DON'T try to handle it yourself – get advice before you reply to the initial letter from the inspector, and at all costs DON'T ring the inspector up to "have a chat and sort this out"
- DON'T ignore it and hope it will go away – penalties are reduced for co-operation and disclosure, not for ignoring the Inspector
- DO be honest and upfront with your Tax Adviser – only then will he or she be able to help you
- DO talk to your accountant about taking out insurance to cover the fees for a tax investigation – the professional fees can be very expensive

16 Inheritance Tax for Property Developers

If you are a property investor or a property developer, you need to consider the impact of Inheritance Tax (IHT).

IHT can be more of a problem for the property investor than for the owners of other types of business – including property developers. This is because property developers, like other trading businesses, will often qualify for Business Property Relief, (see below), which can reduce the IHT on the business assets to nil.

There is a common misconception that IHT is chargeable only when someone dies. In fact, as we shall see, it is also chargeable in certain cases during your lifetime – but this is not always a bad thing!

16.1 IHT – The Basics

IHT is charged on "transfers of value". The commonest "transfer of value" is a gift, but as we shall see later, there are other things which, sometimes unexpectedly, are transfers of value.

When a person dies, they are charged to IHT as if they had made a transfer of value of everything they owned on the day they died. In addition, any transfers of value they made in the seven years ending on the date they died are included.

IHT is charged at the following rates for 2022/23, depending on whether the transfer of value was made during a person's lifetime, or on his or her death:

Transfer of value	Death Rate	Lifetime Rate
0 – 325,000	0%	0%
Above 325,000	40%	20%

The Chancellor announced in Budget 2021 that these bands would be frozen until 2026. Given how property prices continue to rise (and most property specialists seem to be forecasting that property will shake off any contraction brought on by the pandemic relatively quickly) this means that more and more "property-rich" individuals are at risk of being caught by IHT.

16.2 Nil Rate Band (NRB)

The first £325,000, which is charged at 0%, is called the Nil Rate Band ("NRB"). It is often referred to as an "exemption", but this is a misleading way to think about it, as we shall see. Each individual has his or her own NRB.

Transfers to one's spouse or civil partner *are* exempt, and do not use up the deceased's NRB. Basically, if a person leaves everything to their surviving spouse or civil partner, then there will be no IHT. This used to mean that the deceased's NRB was wasted but, since 2007, **the surviving spouse also acquires any NRB that the deceased has not already used against gifts, etc., to other parties**. This means that it is much easier to ensure that both NRBs available to a couple are fully utilised, and it is quite common now to see the second spouse or civil partner have £650,000 (2 x NRB) available on his or her death.

16.3 Residence Nil Rate Band (RNRB)

This is a recent measure, available only on death (unlike the standard NRB, which is also available to cover chargeable lifetime transfers – see below), available with effect from 2017/18, as follows:

- £100,000 in 2017/18
- £125,000 in 2018/19
- £150,000 in 2019/20
- £175,000 in 2020/21

It is available to cover value in the deceased's home, provided it is transferred to direct descendants (children, grandchildren, etc.). It can cover only the value in the home, so can be wasted if the value of the deceased's interest in his home falls short of the RNRB available. Like the 'ordinary' NRB, it is available to each individual, so a couple will have one each.

It follows that, since 2020/21, a married couple/civil partnership has potentially had access to:

2 x (£325,000 + £175,000) = £1million in combined (R)NRBs.

Like the standard NRB, the RNRB is transferrable between spouses and between civil partners; it is possible also to transfer wealth *equivalent* to the home, rather than the property itself, if (for example) the deceased had to go into care prior to death, and the former home had been sold. However, that value equivalent to the RNRB being claimed must still be transferred to direct descendants, in order to qualify. But, simply put, it does mean that there should be more standard NRB left over to cover other assets, such as valuable investments.

Aside from having to ensure that value equivalent to the RNRB being claimed passes only to direct descendants, another key difference between the RNRB and the 'normal' NRB is that **the RNRB can be tapered away** if the chargeable value of the deceased's estate exceeds £2million. (Note that the chargeable value is net of liabilities, such as mortgages). The taper rate is 50%, meaning that the RNRB is reduced by £1 for every £2 by which the deceased's net estate exceeds £2million.

Basic NRB & RNRB

Donald is a wealthy property developer, holding shares in his property company worth £1m, together with a half-share in a palatial residence. Unfortunately, he is taken far too soon in a freak sunbed accident in 2021; his Will leaves everything, including his share in the family home, to his wife, Melissa. There is no IHT on Donald's death, because he has left everything to his spouse. She will acquire Donald's NRB and RNRB, as he has used neither. Melissa carries on the property development business, so it should qualify for Business Property Relief (see later)

When Melissa dies in 2024, she leaves everything (including her home) to her son, Brandon; neither Donald nor Melissa made any lifetime transfers in the 7 years prior to their deaths*.

Value of shares at death	£1,200,000
Add: value of home (net of mortgage)	£1,300,000
Total	£2,500,000
Deduct NRB x 2	(650,000)
RNRB x 2 £350,000 BUT: RNRB Taper - ½ x (£2.5m - £2m) = £250,000 Residual RNRB	(100,000)
	1,750,000
Business Property Relief on Co.	(1,200,000)
Taxable	550,000
IHT Payable (40%)	**220,000**

IHT calculations are almost invariably far more complicated than the above example, but it serves to illustrate the basics maths of the NRB and RNRB. Melissa does not acquire Donald's actual NRB and RNRB that applied on his death, but his unused proportion (in this case 100%) of the Bands that are in point when she later dies.

Melissa's Estate is potentially eligible for 2 x Nil Rate Bands + 2 x Residence Nil Rate Bands, as Donald used neither up to and including his death; only the RNRB is tapered due to the size of Melissa's Estate. If she had not left anything to her son, (or another direct descendant), then no RNRB would have been available at all.

The shares in the company that is eligible for Business Property Relief (see below) are not *in themselves* chargeable to IHT, but they increase the size of Donald's and Melissa's estate for the purposes of calculating her entitlement to the new RNRB. Note that if Donald's estate had been worth more than £2million on its own, then *his* RNRB would have had to be tapered at the point of transfer to Melissa, even though it was not actually used because everything went to Melissa.

In effect, what remains subject to IHT is the main home, net of 2 lots of the standard NRB and the reduced (tapered) RNRB – leaving £550,000 taxable at 40%

16.4 Potentially Exempt Transfers (PETs)

*Not all transfers of value attract IHT when they are made. A simple gift from one individual, during his or her lifetime, to another individual will be a "Potentially Exempt Transfer" ("PET"). This means that if the individual making the gift lives for another seven years after making it, it will fall out of account and no IHT will be charged on it when the individual dies. If, however, they die within seven years, it will form part of their estate at death. We sometimes refer to this as the "seven-year lookback period".

A Failed PET

Joe is a middle aged widower. On 1 April 2022, he makes a cash gift to his son of £100,000, to help him buy a house. This is a PET for IHT purposes, and so there is no IHT to pay at the time. Sadly, during 2023, Joe is killed in a car crash. His estate at death, after deducting all debts, is worth £250,000.

Because Joe has not survived for seven years after making the gift to his son, the PET is added to his estate when calculating the IHT:

Value of estate* at death	250,000
Add gifts in last seven years	100,000
Total	350,000
Deduct NRB*	(325,000)
Chargeable to IHT at 40%	25,000

Note that, if Joe had survived the cash gift to his son by more than 3 years, then the IHT due on the gift would be tapered. (The more years between gift and death, the greater the taper – the taper is effectively 100% after 7 years).

*The Residence Nil Rate Band would be fully in point by 2023: let's assume that Joe acquired his late wife's RNRB in full on her death, (but she had bequeathed £325,000 of her other assets to the children of a previous marriage, so had no NRB left to transfer to Joe) and he also left his home worth exactly 2 x £175,000 = £350,000 to their son so it has been exactly 100% utilised. It has therefore been left out of account both in terms of the value of the chargeable Estate and the corresponding reliefs, to make the above example as simple as possible.

Note that in some circumstances – typically where Trusts have been involved – it may be necessary to look back beyond 7 years prior to death (see 16.8)

16.5 Gifts with Reservation of Benefit

A gift is only a PET if it is really given away. If the person making the gift continues to enjoy a benefit from it, it will be a **"gift with reservation of benefit" ("GWROB").** And will still be treated as owned by the giver, as we shall cover next.

The commonest example of a GWROB is where a parent gifts their house to their child, but continues to live there, but any gift which the giver continues to enjoy will be a GWROB:

GWROB

Sue is a widow, getting on in years, and like many otherwise modestly off people, she has one hugely valuable asset – her house. It is worth £350,000, and the mortgage was paid off long ago. The rest of her assets come to £200,000.

She made a gift of the house to her two children ten years ago, but has continued to live in it. Now she dies, still living in the house.

Because she "reserved a benefit" in the house, by continuing to live in it, for IHT purposes she is treated as if she still owned the house, so the value of her death estate is £550,000. It is irrelevant that she has survived for over seven years since she gave the house away – for IHT purposes it is still hers.

The GWROB rules were sometimes easy to get around, despite numerous tweaks to the legislation over the years. New rules were introduced around a decade ago, that tried to encompass GWROB scenarios. The effect of the relatively new "Pre-Owned Assets Tax" regime is that, if for some reason you are able to circumvent the GWROB regime, then you should – usually, but not always – be subjected to an annual Income Tax charge, broadly based on the rental value of any asset that you continue to enjoy, having legally given it away. The rules for "GWROB" and "POAT" can be complex, particularly in their interaction with each other, and will happily catch innocent transactions where no avoidance was intended or realised. If you think that the rules may apply, then you should get advice.

16.6 Spouse Exemption

A gift or a legacy from one spouse (or civil partner) to the other is exempt from IHT. If you die and leave everything absolutely to your spouse, there will be no IHT to pay, and when their time comes, they will be able to double their Nil Rate Band (and, potentially, Residence Nil Rate Band), because you have not used yours if you have left everything to your spouse or civil partner.

Strictly, this can change if the spouse or civil partner is not "domiciled" in the UK ("domicile" is basically the country one considers to be one's permanent home, and it is in many cases far stickier than merely whichever country one is historically tax-resident). However, since Finance Act 2013, spouses and civil partners can elect to be treated as UK-domiciled even if they are not, which means that in many cases the thorny problem of domicile can be circumvented.

16.7 Business Property Relief

For IHT purposes, "business property" gets relief at either 50% or 100%, depending on its nature. The crucial types of business property for property businesses are:

- An interest in a trading business
- Shares in an unlisted trading company

Unfortunately, a business that substantively includes investments (including investments in rental properties), or dealing in land, does not qualify for BPR.

The two types of business we have looked at in this guide that might qualify for BPR are:

- A property development business – the distinction is between an eligible business where the profits come almost entirely from the development or significant improvement of the property (property development, eligible for BPR), and one where the profit comes to a significant degree from astute buying and selling with minimal work done to the land or properties being traded (dealing in land, and not eligible for BPR). Clearly, this can in many cases be a difficult distinction to make, and you should seek advice if you have any doubts as to which side of the line your business falls

- Furnished Holiday Accommodation (FHA) – this does **not** automatically qualify for BPR, but where the owners are involved in providing services to the holidaymakers (either personally, or through a caretaker or a relative) beyond merely providing the furnished accommodation, then a good case can be made for BPR. If this relief is to be available, the lettings should be short-term only – typically weekly or fortnightly. If the accommodation is let through an agency and there is no contact with the holidaymakers, the position is much more doubtful.

  The simple way to look at the issue is – a hotel *would* normally qualify for BPR, but normal furnished lettings would not, so where on the spectrum between a hotel and a furnished letting does your FHA property come? HMRC have recently started looking more closely at the level of services provided by the FHA, and are likely to challenge claims for BPR unless there is a high level of additional services – shopping, car hire, advice on local amenities, breakfast cooked for the guests, etc. There have been a couple of helpful tax cases in relation to BPR on FHA businesses: **PRs of Graham v HMRC [2018] UK FTT 306** and **Vigne v HMRC [2018] UKUT 0357 (TCC)** – although the second case was actually a livery business, it shares some common ground as HMRC has likewise traditionally resisted claims.

You will appreciate that many property-based businesses will **not** attract BPR, and so the value of the business is likely to be included in your estate on your death, unless you take steps to pass it on during your lifetime. The only good news is that any IHT due on your death which relates to land can be paid in ten annual instalments, rather than being due six months after your death, as is (broadly) the case with IHT on the rest of your estate. This can potentially mean that a property portfolio does not necessarily have to be liquidated in order to pay the IHT liability of the Estate.

16.8 Balancing IHT and CGT

The problem with making lifetime gifts is that the assets that you would like to pass on (because they do not qualify for BPR, so risk increasing the IHT bill) are generally the same ones that you cannot claim CGT holdover relief on (because they are not assets used in a trade – see 11.7), so if you make a gift of them to anyone except your spouse or civil partner, you will be charged to CGT as if you had sold them at market value. (FHAs are the notable exception to this: they may not always be eligible for BPR, but should rank for holdover relief).

In theory, it is absolutely possible for a gift to be chargeable to both CGT at the point of the gift, and subsequently IHT because the donor does not then survive the gift by at least 7 years.

It is even possible for a gift to be chargeable to both CGT and to IHT (at the lifetime rates) at the same time: in the vast majority of cases, a gift will only amount to a Potentially Exempt Transfer – where effectively, HMRC assumes it is exempt but waits for 7 years to make sure – where the gift is from one live individual to another live individual. A gift to a family company or to a Trust will typically attract an immediate lifetime charge to IHT at up to 20%, likely alongside CGT due on the gift.

Fortunately, there is another way to get holdover relief. If a gift is chargeable to IHT as a "lifetime transfer", then any capital gain on that gift can be held over. This is where the "Nil Rate Band" for IHT during one's lifetime becomes important, and potentially useful:

IHT and Holdover for Gifts

Marcus is a widower, and he is not getting any younger, so he wants to pass on his buy-to-let property to his son, Tony. The property cost £150,000 in 1995, and its current market value is £350,000. There is a mortgage of £100,000 secured on it. If Marcus simply gave the property to Tony, he would be deemed to make a capital gain of £200,000, on which he would pay CGT of about £54,000 after his annual exempt amount.

Instead, Marcus sets up a Trust, with Tony as the beneficiary, and transfers the property to the Trust, on condition that the Trust takes over the mortgage secured on the property (to which the mortgagee helpfully agrees).

In order to be a PET a gift must be to an individual, and a Trust is not an individual, so the gift to a Trust is a "Chargeable Lifetime Transfer" for IHT purposes. So, this transfer is *potentially* chargeable to both IHT and to CGT

In order to find the amount of IHT payable, we look at how much Marcus' Estate has reduced as a result of the gift. He is poorer by the value of the property (£350,000), but richer by no longer owing £100,000 on the mortgage, so the total loss to his Estate is £250,000, and that is the amount chargeable to IHT.

Looking at the rates for IHT (see the beginning of this section) we find that the first £325,000 is charged at 0% (the "Nil Rate Band"), so no IHT is actually payable. Because the transfer is <u>chargeable</u> to IHT, however, Marcus (and the Trustees of the Trust) can make a claim to hold over the capital gain on the transfer. Marcus has used £250,000 of his £325,000 Nil Rate Band, but seven years after the date of this gift, it drops out of account and he can make another gift in a similar manner (and rest assured, Marcus had made no gifts in the 7 years before this transfer, either).

NOTE: Marcus makes the gift to "a Trust". There are several different kinds of Trust, and Marcus should take advice from a Tax Adviser before deciding what sort of Trust to use. This is very much an area for experts, and there are likely to be disastrous consequences if you do not take specialist advice before embarking on a strategy of this nature.

For example, if the Trustees have taken on responsibility for the mortgage, then this may count as "chargeable consideration" for the purposes of SDLT – in other words, SDLT may be due on the transfer into Trust (see 14.6). **Likewise, where Chargeable Lifetime Transfers are involved, the 7-year look-back period from death can be extended to 14 years** (see also 16.4).

There are other strategies for mitigating IHT, and property developers who want to be able to pass their businesses and other assets down the generations need to take early advice– as you will have seen from *Marcus*, this sort of planning can be a long-term project, involving seven-year gaps between transfers.

Congratulations – You've now finished 'Tax Tips for Property Developers and Renovators'

To learn even more ways on how to legitimately cut your property tax bills please visit: www.property-tax-portal.co.uk.

Milton Keynes UK
Ingram Content Group UK Ltd.
UKHW051056171223
434437UK00026B/595